THE INTERNATIONAL CONSULTANT

H. Peter Guttmann

THE INTERNATIONAL CONSULTANT

Revised Edition

International Law Institute     John Wiley & Sons, Inc.

International Law Institute
1330 Connecticut Avenue, N.W.
Washington, D.C. 20036
(202)463-7979

Library of Congress Catalog No.: 87-61545

ISBN 0-471-60911-0

Printed and bound in the United States of America

10 9 8 7 6 5 4 3 2 1

TABLE OF CONTENTS

INTRODUCTION

In writing this book, I have envisioned consultants in a broad way: as architects, economists, educators, engineers, managers, and planners. Some may work as individuals, some as members of small teams in highly specialized areas of professional expertise, while others might belong to firms, the size and nature of which can fall within a wide spectrum. What unites this concept of *consultant* is the diversity of the engagements they undertake, and, particularly in the case of work outside the highly industrialized or so-called post-industrial countries, the orientation toward "development" work. Thus consulting, as I shall speak of it, encompasses projects in agriculture, commerce, communications, energy, industry, applied environmental science, and transportation.

I write as an engineer with a long career in engineering/consulting that has taken me to many well-known and to some very remote places throughout the world. During these years my work has been related in one way or another to numerous professions beyond strict engineering and the practicing engineer. For nearly ten years now my private practice in Washington has become increasingly varied, with emphasis on the many issues and technicalities of financing international development projects. Most recently, teaching at the International Law Institute has greatly expanded my contact with and appreciation of the other side of the consultant's fence—that of the client. My perspective derives primarily from these experiences, and I would like to think that what I have learned from them permits me to venture some helpful observations about the extensive subject of international consulting.

Success in the international field depends very much on qualifications, and this fact places great selective pressure on specialization. Somewhat paradoxically, then, this book is not a specialist's work, at least not within a given profession or in the sense of having a narrow focus. My intention, rather, is to address the more general concerns of the practitioners of several professions who wish to carry their expertise into the world at large. In particular, I have tried to provide guidance for consultants contemplating or actually making their debut on the international scene. Those also established in international practice should still find material with which to review their approaches and policies. And this is appropriate, for the role of the consultant is always evolving.

Consultants once functioned primarily as advisors. Soon after the turn of the century, the skills required by ever larger and more complex projects quickly exceeded the capabilities of any individual or firm. Thereupon the specialist who consulted became engaged in the actual execution of work such as studies, reports, design, specification, supervision, project management, training, and even the administration and management of facilities. Few consultants, whether firms or individuals, can now survive solely on the base of narrow expertise. Instead, the nature of present development work demands the integration of technical subjects with socioeconomic factors, environmental concerns, and financing. Nationalistic tendencies have often limited undertakings to consultants of one country, speaking the same language—that of their clients or a historically related one. Now, however, international teams with members from numerous countries and speaking several languages are becoming common and require considerable professional flexibility.

Flexibility, indeed, is a virtue in working with people in places and conditions that may differ sharply from one's home. Just these inevitable differences that characterize so much of international work also place a premium on the related virtues of tolerance, sensitivity, and articulateness. A consultant will never be successful internationally by simply producing technically accurate work; the work must also be well communicated, which is a rather different matter. It is my further conviction that consultants should adhere to the highest standards of professional ethics. This requires that they remain independent of all suppliers and manufacturers, and that there is no room for payoffs and kickbacks at home or abroad.

The international market for consulting services is highly competitive, but also very large. World-wide consulting is a multimillion dollar industry. Consulting, as a whole, is a business, not philanthropy. While it would be naive to overlook the profit motive that inspires professional efforts, it is necessary to retain sight of the fact that the professional services that architects, planners, engineers, economists, and other consultants render in many ways underpin the physical workings of the societies that pay for them. This is a large responsibility and leads me to assert that the importance of the uses to which the specialist's knowledge is put as it is translated into various projects around the world entails a distinct obligation of honesty and precision.

Some readers may be disappointed by the absence of draft contract forms. These might be helpful to a modest extent; however, actual circumstances present so many special considerations that an attempt to represent this important type of document by an individual sample, or even several, would be unwise. Although many clients are presently using forms that approach uniformity, contract language remains a matter for legal counsel.

Finally, I would like to apologize for my persistent use of masculine pronouns. This usage reflects ingrained linguistic habit, not lack of respect for the significant number of women who are practicing internationally with success and distinction.

H. Peter Guttmann
Washington, D.C.

THE
INTERNATIONAL
CONSULTANT

1

COMPETING IN THE WORLD MARKET

The world market offers enormous opportunities and challenges to the international consultant. There is more than enough work in the international marketplace to keep all the established consultants in the world busy for the next twenty-five years. But because of political considerations and economic difficulties, only a fraction of this work will be commissioned, and that fraction will go to those professional consultants who are aggressive, well prepared, and can count on support from their own governments. Sovereign governments, powerful international financiers, nationals from many countries, and some of the world's most renowned professionals vie with each other in a fiercely competitive market.

The marketplace for international consultants includes all the nations of the globe: 189 sovereign countries and territories whose populations range from less than 150 thousand to more than a billion. These prospective markets comprise industrial and developing nations, different political and economic systems, the world's major language groups and religions affiliations, and income levels that vary markedly even among countries in the same geographic area.

Consultants who are thoroughly informed about specific regional markets begin with a distinct advantage. Fortunately, this information is not hard to find. One good source is the atlas published annually by the World Bank, which contains not only maps, but data on population, gross national product, gross national product per capita, life expectancy, infant mortality, and primary-school enrollment. The smart consultant knows what a potential client needs.

1

Countries working to develop a fundamental infrastructure and the basic components of a modern economy will seek individuals and firms with the technical knowledge they need. Countries lacking money and organizational skills will seek specialists in investment financing and management services. This sounds simple enough, but bringing those who have knowledge—the engineers, architects, and other specialists—together with the governments, national institutions, or private organizations that need their expertise is difficult to achieve. Human affairs are complicated by politics, economics, and ideological and cultural differences.

Political competition is as ferocious as business competition. Local wars seem endemic throughout the world, and conflict between the United States and the Soviet Union insinuates itself into every region where the two superpowers seek to extend their spheres of influence. These conflicts complicate all forms of exchange, not only between capitalist and socialist economies, but among virtually all participants in the global economy. The international monetary system itself is an imperfect structure vulnerable to intricate manipulations and subject to enormous strains. Everyone now recognizes that the practices of development that followed World War II have not been uniformly wise or equitable and that the pattern of life and technology evolving in the United States and Europe may not be universally welcome or successful in all cultures. These considerations cloud the theoretical model of supply and demand, from which point even international consultants must still take their first step.

When knowledge and technology are for sale, common sense would seem to make expertise, experience, and availability the primary criteria for selection. To the degree that reason rules international trade, they generally are. But the rule of reason is precarious, and, as they have for centuries, matters of politics and religion claim a significant place in many transactions. Players in the game of international prejudice change, but the game itself seems to go on without any signs of ending.

The consultant venturing into the international scene confronts the paradox that some things in international affairs are very simple and some very complex; that international commerce, while premised on stability, always retains the potential for volatility. To survive in this world, let alone profit in it, requires insight, discretion, and flexibility.

The International Market: A Regional Perspective

Before doing anything, the consultant must have a basic understanding of local conditions in countries and regions that are potential markets. The following statistics have been taken from *The World Bank Annual Report 1987*. The International Bank for Reconstruction and Development (IBRD), or World Bank as it is generally known, has, through 1986, categorized borrowers in the emerging nations according to six geographical groupings: Eastern and Southern Africa; Western Africa; East Asia and the Pacific; South Asia; Europe, Middle East and North Africa; and Latin America and the Caribbean. (In mid-1987 the Bank reorganized itself in order to focus more sharply on the needs of individual member nations. One result of the reorganization is the consolidation of the six regions into four: Africa; Asia; Europe, the Middle East, and North Africa; and Latin America and the Caribbean. Future annual reports of the Bank will present its regional perspectives within that new framework.)

The country-by-country data compiled by the Bank are essential background information for consultants in every field. The material that follows will give you a sense of the magnitude of the world market for international consultant services.

Eastern and Southern Africa

The twenty-one countries of Eastern and Southern Africa rely heavily on exporting a few primary products to earn the foreign exchange they need to pay for their imports.

Since 1980, much economic hardship in the area has been caused by prolonged drought and sustained declines in the prices of regional exports. During fiscal 1987, the region's economic situation improved, primarily because the weather was more benign, but also because policy reforms in some countries began to yield benefits. Nevertheless, prolonged cuts in consumption and investment have damaged the productive base in several economies; the servicing of external debt represents a heavy, if not sometimes unmanageable, burden for some; and the long-term prospects for most primary exports remain gloomy.

In part because of ample rainfall, agricultural production increased in almost every country. Zimbabwe, in particular, had exportable food surpluses. Botswana, Lesotho, and Mozambique are expected to require further emergency food aid in 1987/88. The

Eastern and Southern Africa:
1985 Population and Per Capita GNP of
Country Borrowers, Fiscal Years 1985–87

Country Borrowers, FY 1985–87	Population[a] (thousands)	Per Capita GNP 1985[b] (US$)
Botswana	1,070	840
Burundi	4,696	230
Comoros	454	240
Djibouti	362	n.a.
Ethiopia	42,271	110
Kenya	20,375	290
Lesotho	1,545	470
Madagascar	10,212	240
Malawi	7,044	170
Mauritius	1,020	1,090
Mozambique	13,791	160
Rwanda	6,026	280
Seychelles	65	n.a.
Somalia	5,384	280
Sudan	21,931	300
Swaziland	757	670
Tanzania[c]	22,242	290
Uganda	14,680	n.a.
Zaire	30,557	170
Zambia	6,704	390
Zimbabwe	8,406	680

NOTE: The 1985 estimates of GNP per capita presented above are from the "World Development Indicators" in the *World Development Report 1987*.

n.a. Not available.
a. Estimates for mid–1985.
b. *World Bank Atlas* methodology, 1983–85 base period.
c. The GNP per capita refers to mainland Tanzania only.

Source: *The World Bank Annual Report 1987*

continuing high rates of population growth, however, meant that only four countries—Somalia, Burundi, Tanzania, and Zaire—reported increases in per capita income in 1986. Per capita income fell in Botswana, Kenya, Lesotho, Madagascar, Malawi, Sudan, Swaziland, Zambia, and Zimbabwe.

Despite the fact that average prices for imports rose slightly, the region's external terms of trade improved by 5 percent during 1986, and the inflow of foreign resources into the region in 1986 also declined. The sharp decline in the price of oil will save many of the countries substantial amounts of foreign exchange. Higher coffee prices benefit exporters from Burundi, Ethiopia, Kenya, Madagascar, Rwanda, Tanzania, Uganda, and Zaire. If copper and sugar prices rise slightly in this period, the region would also benefit.

As will be noted from the above, the economic condition of the Eastern and Southern Africa region is a precarious one.

Western Africa

The general outlook for Western Africa is not particularly encouraging. While the return of good rainfall generated higher levels of food production than in the past few years, many critical constraints to adjustment and longer-term development have not yet been overcome. The Cote d'Ivoire (Ivory Coast) and Ghana have reinforced their ongoing stabilization, and Guinea, Niger, and Senegal continue to show improvements in their agricultural and industrial sectors. Progress in The Gambia and Mauritania in this connection is quite impressive. But the rapid overall population growth coupled with general budget austerity represents a generally oppressive burden. Important exports of the region, such as cotton, iron ore, uranium, and groundnuts, could all continue to be adversely affected by prices. This is of major concern to Benin, Burkina Faso, the Central African Republic, Chad, The Gambia, Liberia, Mali, Niger, Mauritania, and Senegal. On the other hand, oil-exporting countries such as Cameroon, the People's Republic of the Congo, Gabon, and Nigeria are suffering from the sharp slump and continuing instability in world oil prices.

In 1986, Cameroon experienced a devastating natural disaster which set back some of the ongoing undertakings and limited funding of some projects planned for the future. Nigeria, Africa's most populous nation, is struggling hard to meet the needs of her exploding population. Consultant services are continuously required by Lagos, yet local politics, internal economics and international finan-

cial limitations make the Nigerian marketplace one of the most
difficult in the world for professional consultants.

Western Africa:
1985 Population and Per Capita GNP of
Country Borrowers, Fiscal Years 1985–87

Country Borrowers, FY 1985–87	Population[a] (thousands)	Per Capita GNP 1985[b] (US$)
Benin	4,043	260
Burkina Faso	7,885	150
Cameroon	10,191	810
Cape Verde	325	430
Central African Republic	2,583	260
Chad	5,018	n.a.
Congo, People's Republic of the	1,872	1,110
Côte d'Ivoire	10,072	660
Equatorial Guinea	373	n.a.
Gambia, The	748	230
Ghana	12,710	380
Guinea	6,166	320
Guinea-Bissau	886	180
Liberia	2,204	470
Mali	7,511	150
Mauritania	1,693	420
Niger	6,391	250
Nigeria	99,669	800
São Tomé and Principe	108	320
Senegal	6,567	370
Sierra Leone	3,657	350
Togo	3,038	230

NOTE: The 1985 estimates of GNP per capita presented above are
from the "World Development Indicators" in the *World Development Report 1987*.

n.a. Not available.
a. Estimates for mid–1985.
b. *World Bank Atlas* methodology, 1983–85 base period.

Source: *The World Bank Annual Report 1987*

East Asia and Pacific

The countries of the East Asia and Pacific regions have fared remarkably well during the past two decades. Although the growth rate of the gross national product (GNP) in Indonesia, Malaysia, the Philippines, and Thailand has slowed somewhat since the 1970s, growth is continuing, but at the price of an increased burden of external debt. By far the most important country of the region is the People's Republic of China. With the world's largest population (more than one billion people) and a per capita GNP of $310, the

East Asia and Pacific:
1985 Population and Per Capita GNP of
Country Borrowers, Fiscal Years 1985–87

Country Borrowers, FY 1985–87	Population[a] (thousands)	Per Capita GNP 1985[b] (US$)
China	1,040,338	310
Fiji	696	1,710
Indonesia	162,212	530
Korea, Republic of	41,056	2,150
Lao People's Democratic Republic	3,609	n.a.
Malaysia	15,571	2,000
Papua New Guinea	3,511	680
Philippines	54,725	580
Solomon Islands	267	510
Thailand	51,700	800
Tonga	97	730
Vanuatu	134	880
Western Samoa	163	660

NOTE: The 1985 estimates of GNP per capita presented above are from the "World Development Indicators" in the *World Development Report 1987*.

n.a. Not available.
a. Estimates for mid–1985.
b. *World Bank Atlas* methodology, 1983–85 base period.

Source: *The World Bank Annual Report 1987*.

Chinese economy is moving ahead at a strong pace; the real national income rose in 1986 by 7.8 percent, after a slowdown in the first half of the year. Highly industrialized, with a vast agricultural potential and almost unlimited human resources, China is developing in all sectors. Consultants, therefore, are much in demand and it is generally accepted that China is today one of the world's most challenging marketplaces for consulting services.

Korea is another example of rapid development. A recipient of soft loans from the international financial community in the 1950s, this country today is a major exporter of goods and equipment, competing successfully against Japan, Taiwan, Hong Kong, and Singapore. While still an active market for consulting services, Korea is also starting to offer Koreans as consultants in several areas of professional endeavor.

Indonesia, suffering from declining and unstable oil prices, is another very active marketplace for consulting services. Here a mix of local/domestic and international/foreign talent is greatly in demand.

Recent political events in the Philippines have temporarily paralyzed many of the programs that involved substantial consultant services from many parts of the world and in many sectors. Nevertheless, the nation is expected gradually to overcome the present difficulties and if all goes well, the Philippine marketplace will open up again within the next few years.

Papua New Guinea, one of the young countries in the area, shows a decline in GNP of approximately 4 percent in 1987. Medium-term development plans prepared by the government should accentuate the need for consulting services in many sectors of the country's infrastructure.

The city-state of Singapore is not included in the World Bank's report because Singapore's economy is well advanced. This highly industrialized and extraordinarily well-organized republic, with a population of 2.5 million, is modern, progressive and highly international in character. Singapore, which shows a constructive ethic of a progressive, economically responsible and socially oriented government, is an Asian showcase for the development of public works, modern transportation systems, the latest in convertible waste disposal techniques, communications, schools and centers for higher education. Logically, Singapore avails itself of consultants with specialized knowledge in such high-tech areas as research and development (R&D), industrial development, and communications systems.

South Asia

The economies of the seven countries comprising the South Asian region depend to a large extent on the performance of their agricultural sectors. In recent years, they have benefitted from good growing conditions and economic stability in major consumer countries. India, Pakistan and Sri Lanka have achieved virtual self-sufficiency in food grains, while Bangladesh has made such progress that the need for food grain imports may no longer exist by the end of the decade. In Burma major advances have been made in the expanding production of paddy. Although there was a slackening in 1986, South Asia as a whole shows a steady pattern of growth; gross domestic product (GDP) during the 1980s has increased over 4 percent each year. India's performance, particularly, is impressive. Despite heavy population increases and deep-seated religious and political difficulties, the country is progressing very much in the industrial sector and is becoming a major producer and

South Asia:
1985 Population and Per Capita GNP of
Country Borrowers, Fiscal Years 1985–87

Country Borrowers, FY 1985–87	*Population*[a] *(thousands)*	*Per Capita GNP 1985*[b] *(US$)*
Bangladesh	100,592	150
Bhutan	1,240	160
Burma	36,943	190
India	765,147	270
Nepal	16,527	160
Pakistan	96,180	380
Sri Lanka	15,837	380

NOTE: The 1985 estimates of GNP per capita presented above are from the "World Development Indicators" in the *World Development Report 1987*.

n.a. Not available.
a. Estimates for mid–1985.
b. *World Bank Atlas* methodology, 1983–85 base period.

Source: *The World Bank Annual Report 1987*

exporter of materials and industrial equipment. Bangladesh also shows improvement over 1986. Both Bangladesh and Pakistan, incidentally, are major users of consulting services from abroad. Burma, Sri Lanka, and Nepal had declining rates of growth in fiscal 1986, although they were still positive in per capita terms. However, Burma's visible recovery since 1980 is somewhat obscured by serious financial imbalances which are currently causing reductions in expenditures and imports. Sri Lanka and Nepal are aiming at boosting exports in order to earn needed foreign exchange. Sri Lanka is in the middle of an ambitious public investment program, highlighted by the major works associated with the Mahaweli irrigation and power development scheme, which helped to create the basis for sustaining the country's long-term growth. In the short-term, however, the recent downturn in tea, coconut, and rubber prices has created strains that are evident in major sectors of the economy, particularly, of course, the export sector.

Nepal, one of the poorest countries in the world, nevertheless is undertaking as many infrastructural development projects as her limited budget and international donors can commit to. Like Bangladesh and Pakistan, Sri Lanka and Nepal are and will remain continuous users of international consulting services.

Europe, Middle East, and North Africa

Not included in the World Bank statistics are the industrial nations of Europe or the large petroleum exporters of the Middle East—Saudi Arabia, Kuwait, Libya, and the United Arab Emirates.

The fourteen countries in the region who work with and receive assistance from the World Bank range from the very poor, such as the Yemen Arab Republic and the People's Democratic Republic of Yemen, to countries regarded as semi-industrial, such as Hungary, Portugal, Turkey, and Yugoslavia. Afghanistan, which has traditionally been one of the poorer countries in the area, is, since the invasion by the Soviet Union, no longer accessible to free market forces and has not been known to be interested in foreign consulting services. Iran and Iraq, two major nations in the area, continue to be locked in a devastating war, severely restricting the once encouraging possibilities for development work in their territories. Jordan and Egypt, both heavily supported by international donors through the extension of development assistance funds, are prime markets for consulting services with substantial projects in many sectors. Israel, on the other hand, also extensively subsidized, has very

**Europe, Middle East, and North Africa:
1985 Population and Per Capita GNP of
Country Borrowers, Fiscal Years 1985–87**

Country Borrowers, FY 1985–87	Population[a] (thousands)	Per Capita GNP 1985[b] (US$)
Algeria	21,905	2,550
Cyprus	665	3,790
Egypt, Arab Republic of	48,503	610
Hungary	10,649	1,950
Jordan	3,505	1,560[c]
Morocco	21,925	560
Oman	1,242	6,730
Portugal	10,229	1,970
Syrian Arab Republic	10,505	1,570
Tunisia	7,143	1,190
Turkey	50,248	1,080
Yemen, Arab Republic	7,955	550
Yemen, People's Democratic Republic of	2,086	530
Yugoslavia	23,123	2,070

NOTE: The 1985 estimates of GNP per capita presented above are from the "World Development Indicators" in the *World Development Report 1987*.

n.a. Not available.
a. Estimates for mid–1985.
b. *World Bank Atlas* methodology, 1983–85 base period.
c. East Bank only.

Source: *The World Bank Annual Report 1987*

little need for outside consultants and, in fact, is a major exporter of consultancy services.

During the past two decades, petroleum has sparked, in the Middle East, the greatest development activities the world has ever witnessed. Hundreds of consultants have been performing professional services in Saudi Arabia, Kuwait, the United Arab Emirates, and a few other countries. However, with the decline of oil prices, it is obvious that the unprecedented development activity in the region has come to an end. Consulting services required in the area will shift from planning, design, and supervision of construction to education, training, management, and other human resources-related fields.

Central economic planning in Hungary and Yugoslavia has yielded some sporadic progress but also led to occasional domestic difficulties, particularly by severely increasing foreign debt. Libya, currently regarded as an outlaw state within the United States' sphere of influence, has sharply decreased her commerce with the free world. Uncertain political conditions have slowed investments in Greece and Cyprus. However, the economic recovery of Turkey during the past several years has led to development activities that are nothing short of spectacular. Turkish plans for development in her power and transportation sectors alone can be regarded as unique in today's world.

Europe, the Middle East, and North Africa have been the most active markets for major consulting services since the early 1970s. While no major increase in professional services demands may be anticipated, as a whole the region will continue to need great numbers of qualified individuals and firms that offer professional services, especially in the fields of management, training, maintenance, and repair. The Middle East, in particular, has never been an easy area to work in. However, many consultants have found that project work there, despite exceptional difficulties and risks, has been challenging and profitable.

Latin America and the Caribbean

In Latin America, economic growth rates of between 5 percent and 8.5 percent were achieved by Peru, Brazil, Argentina, Chile, Colombia, and Uruguay. Output on a per capita basis of most Latin American countries declined or stagnated.

Deep social and political problems continue to impede prosperity in Central and South America. The most obvious and best known obstacle, because of its effects on the solvency of significant segments of the American-European system, is the staggering debt problem of countries such as Argentina, Brazil, Mexico, Peru, and Venezuela. The International Monetary Fund, the World Bank, groups of commercial bankers, entrepreneurs, as well as the central banks of the industrial nations are all engaged in a high stakes game with the governments of these and other Latin nations attempting to find solutions for the reduction of debts. Despite many well-publicized efforts to the contrary, local capital still escapes into

Latin America and the Caribbean:
1985 Population and Per Capita GNP of
Country Borrowers, Fiscal Years 1985–87

Country Borrowers, FY 1985–87	Population[a] (thousands)	Per Capita GNP 1985[b] (US$)
Argentina	30,531	2,130
Bahamas	231	7,070
Barbados	254	4,630
Belize	159	1,190
Bolivia	6,383	470
Brazil	135,564	1,640
Chile	12,074	1,430
Colombia	28,418	1,320
Costa Rica	2,600	1,300
Dominica	78	1,150
Dominican Republic	6,416	790
Ecuador	9,378	1,160
Grenada	96	970
Guatemala	7,963	1,250
Guyana	790	500
Haiti	5,922	310
Honduras	4,383	720
Jamaica	2,227	940
Mexico	78,820	2,080
Panama	2,180	2,100
Paraguay	3,693	860
Peru	·18,612	1,010
Uruguay	3,012	1,650

NOTE: The 1985 estimates of GNP per capita presented above are from the "World Development Indicators" in the *World Development Report 1987.*

n.a. Not available.
a. Estimates for mid–85.
b. *World Bank Atlas* methodology, 1983–85 base period.

Source: *The World Bank Annual Report 1987*

the money markets of the United States and Switzerland where relatively low interest is being earned. It is impossible to say if guarantees against expropriation and nationalization, the lifting of official restrictions on money transfers, and less taxation will finally succeed to stem the outflow and, in fact, stimulate local investment in Latin America by the Latin Americans themselves, where much higher rates of interest can be earned than in North America and Europe. It is certain, however, that the kind of situation described above does lead to continuous unrest and chronic and acute crises.

This does not mean that development of the vast agricultural, labor, and industrial resources of the area will come to a halt. There is still a great need for infrastructure, housing, health care, education, transportation, communications, and energy in most of these countries. But, as in Africa, social and political problems are compounded by economies undermined by general instability and weak world markets for traditional agricultural products, minerals, and ores. Lower petroleum prices have favored the economies of some of the nonexporting countries while hurting others; but rising coffee prices during the past year may bring temporary relief to some sectors in Guatemala, Costa Rica, Colombia, and Brazil.

Guatemala is still recovering from a devastating earthquake in the 1970s; Mexico was very hard hit by such a natural disaster in 1986, as was El Salvador during the second half of 1986. Altogether, despite impressive accomplishments by most of the countries of the region in achieving external adjustments, there has been very little progress, and economic recession and crisis continue in much of Latin America.

Although almost all of the Caribbean countries showed recovery in 1985, they did not sustain the economic advances that had been predicted in years past. In the Caribbean, tourism increased slightly. Demands for regional exports such as oil, bauxite, sugar, and manufactures remained weak. Unemployment has grown and foreign exchange shortages have increased. An ambitious program by the government of the United States to assist the area (the Caribbean Basin Initiative, or C.B.I.) so far has not produced any noticeable results whatsoever.

Central and South America have long provided challenging and profitable work for consultants and, despite increasingly difficult conditions, the need for such services continues. Professionals should expect to compete with highly educated and experienced Latin Americans. Competitive consulting services are now being offered by local individuals and firms. This is a development that requires new and quite different approaches and I will discuss them later.

A Bird's Eye View of International Markets

While still lucrative, the market for international consultants has decreased slightly in the last five years. Foreign billings by the world's top 200 international design firms in 1986 were $3.54 billion, 8 percent below the peak year of 1983. This decline has been caused by budget cuts in the OPEC countries, Third World debt and financing problems, and increased demand by developing countries for use of local labor and material resources. It is important to keep these factors in mind, because LDC markets (the Middle East, Asia, Africa, and Latin America) account for over 85 percent of international billings.

Since the early 1980s there has also been a substantial shift in the regions considered to be the growth areas for international consulting in design work. In 1982 Middle Eastern billings accounted for 34 percent of total international billings by the top 200 firms. By 1986 the Middle Eastern market was 28 percent smaller, and the Latin American market had shrunk by 16 percent. Asia, on the other hand, had become the primary growth market, reaching billings of $982 million in 1986, a 34 percent increase over 1982. Figures for consultant payments compiled annually by *ENR* magazine (formerly *Engineering News Record*) give us a useful picture of which countries receive the lion's share of consulting contracts. (All figures in this section are taken from *ENR*, August 6, 1987.)

Middle East

Assignments in Middle Eastern countries generated a total of $907 million in billings from international architectural and engineering consultants in 1986. Of this, $272 million went to 42 U.S. firms; $160 million to 26 British firms; $89 million to 16 German firms; $79 million to 8 Swiss firms; and $53 million to 8 Dutch firms.

While the income of the major petroleum exporting nations in the Middle East has declined dramatically in the past few years, there are still many major development projects in the planning stage or on the drawing board. New facilities being completed, and others beginning to operate, will require considerable services from consultants in the areas of training, operations, and maintenance. The major countries in the area—Saudi Arabia, Kuwait, the United Arab Emirates, Oman, Qatar, and their neighbors—will constitute a major market for international consultants during the next several years. Remember that the enormous amount of basic infrastructure construction in the Middle East (ports and harbors; roads and highways; schools and hospitals) has been followed by technologically sophisticated projects in transportation systems, air-port design and construction, desalination, chemical and industrial engineering, and communications. It is safe to predict that much of the work in the Middle East in the 1980s and well beyond is likely to require state-of-the-art technology comparable to projects in the most advanced industrial nations. The following countries belong in that category:

Bahrain	Oman
Egypt	Qatar
Iraq	Saudi Arabia
Israel	Syria
Jordan	Turkey
Kuwait	United Arab Emirates

Asia

Only fifteen years ago there was practically no relationship be-tween the United States and the People's Republic of China. Today, many hundreds of millions of dollars flow from east to west, mostly as payment for technology and know-how exported to the east. Relatively few private consultants have been successful in offering professional services in socialist countries, as the demand has been for turn-key contractors and industrial corporations able to deliver entire petrochemical, steel, and other mechanical facilities, prefera-bly packaged with favorable financing. If some of the philosophical divergence between East and West is lessened, which may well happen, it is clear that the Soviet Union and several of the socialist and people's republics will emerge as vast markets for consultants from the Western world.

Japan has emerged during the past three decades as a unique force in development. In many ways the most efficient indus-trialized country in the world, Japan today exercises a dominant commercial influence in Asia and her economic power is felt throughout the world. Japan itself is only marginally open to or in need of foreign consulting services, and fields only a limited conven-tional consulting profession. But Japanese technological capability has infiltrated the traditional domains of consulting practice through industrial combines and superbly organized state-assisted trading companies.

Asian projects generated a total of $982 million in billings for architectural and engineering firms in 1986. Of this, $236 million went to 41 U.S. firms; $196 million to 26 British firms; $157 million to 12 Japanese firms; $52 million to 11 Canadian firms; and $105 million to 8 Dutch firms.

Consulting work in Asia encompasses the entire range of professional services, from pre-investment studies through management training and the operation of high-tech facilities. The most tantalizing prospect in Asia is the People's Republic of China. As China is changing into a modern industrial nation, consultants will play an important role in assisting its development.

Indonesia is another market that needs, and is well able to absorb and use, advice and guidance from international consultants. India has matured as a major agricultural and industrial producer to the extent that Indian professionals are beginning to provide international consulting services. At the same time, India continues to receive as much transfer of know-how as she can afford and absorb. Malaysia and Thailand are attractive countries in which to work, as is Pakistan. Even Bangladesh, one of the poorest nations in the world, is an active consumer of technology to improve her people's standard of life. During 1986, the following countries engaged major international architectural and engineering consulting firms:

Bangladesh	Korea, South
Brunei	Malaysia
Burma	Nepal
China (People's Republic of China)	Pacific Islands
	Papua New Guinea
Fiji	Singapore
Hong Kong	Sri Lanka
India	Taiwan
Indonesia	Thailand
Japan	Vietnam

Africa

Africa contracted for $855 million in services from architectural and engineering firms in 1986. Of this, $125 million went to 29 U.S. firms; $98 million to 21 British firms; $157 million to 15 French firms; $120 million to 20 German firms; and $68 million to 7 Dutch firms.

While Africa does not match the market potential of Asia, especially for sophisticated consulting services, it does constitute a major market for consultants in practically all areas of professional expertise. With the exception of South Africa, virtually all the nations of Africa require extensive development assistance.

Nigeria, with a population of more than 100 million, has been a strong market for foreign know-how during the past two decades. Richly endowed with human and natural resources, Nigeria is well on the way to becoming one of the African continent's most important nations by the end of this century, given stable political conditions and competent economic management.

Despite the consequences of the devastating drought in the sub-
Sahara region, much work will be done in Africa. In 1985, international architectural and engineering consultants were engaged in
the following countries:

Algeria	Libya
Angola	Malawi
Benin	Morocco
Botswana	Mozambique
Burkina Faso	Nigeria
Burundi	Rwanda
Cameroon	Senegal
Cape Verde	Sierra Leone
Congo	Somalia
Egypt	South Africa
Ethiopia	Sudan
Gabon	Swaziland
Gambia	Tanzania
Ghana	Tunisia
Guinea	Uganda
Ivory Coast	Upper Volta
Kenya	Zaire
Lesotho	Zambia
Liberia	Zimbabwe

Europe

Europe produced $314 million in revenues for architectural and
engineering firms in 1986. Of this, $113 million went to 30 U.S.
firms; $58 million to 8 Scandinavian firms; $43 million to 12 French
firms; $17 million to 17 British firms; and $30 million to 6 Swiss
consulting firms.

While Europe is commonly grouped with North America and
Japan as a primary source of advanced technology, the European
nations of Greece, Portugal, Spain and Yugoslavia are still in need
of technical and educational development assistance. Also, the
highly industrialized free-market economies of the European countries listed below offer opportunities for sophisticated consulting
services:

Austria	Denmark
Belgium	Germany, West

France   Scandinavia
Ireland   Switzerland
Italy   United Kingdom
Netherlands

Much of the work deals with advanced transportation and communication systems; air and water pollution abatement and other areas of environmental research and protection; energy generation, particularly energy conservation in industrial plants; and computer applications and information processing. Clearly only the cream of high-specialization foreign consultants will find an opportunity to participate in this work.

Latin America

Latin American billings from architectural and engineering consultants amounted to $321 million in 1986. Of this, $160 million went to 31 U.S. firms; $28 million to 13 Canadian firms; $18 million to 13 German firms; and $24 million to 7 Scandinavian consulting companies.

The foreign debt crisis of the Latin countries has derailed many major new development projects. The need for consultants will not disappear, but the ability to finance them and the projects they serve will remain problematic well into the immediate future. During 1984, architectural and engineering consultants worked in:

Argentina   Guyana
Bolivia   Honduras
Brazil   Mexico
Chile   Nicaragua
Colombia   Panama
Costa Rica   Paraguay
Ecuador   Peru
El Salvador   Uruguay
Guatemala   Venezuela

North America

Strange as it may seem, the United States and Canada, two of the world's major suppliers of architectural and engineering services, attract large numbers of foreign consultants. Many of these firms arrive in the new world as professional associates of domestic specialists; others incorporate as new domestic entities, or purchase existing firms. Internal competition and legal and professional requirements are rigorous, but the United States and Canada are open to foreign expertise.

North American architectural and engineering consulting services totaled $161 million in 1986, with $85 million going to 10 Canadian firms working in the United States; $13 million to 13 U.S. firms working in Canada; $19 million to 4 Swiss firms; and $5 million to 4 Scandinavian consulting companies.

Australia and New Zealand

The internal development of both countries has produced first class architects, engineers, and planners who not only meet the greater part of their own national needs, but also compete as consultants to the entire world market. Nonetheless, some highly specialized or extremely large projects do require foreign participation. As in the case of Europe, only those firms with the highest qualifications and the most competitive stance are likely to succeed in penetrating the Australia/New Zealand market.

International Competition

Whose consultants play in the big leagues? Mainly firms from the United States, Scandinavia, Switzerland, Italy, England, Germany, the Netherlands, Belgium, France, Canada, and Spain. Consultants from Portugal tend to confine their international work to former colonies—Brazil, Angola, Mozambique—where their language is spoken. Belgians find work principally in French-speaking countries, Zaire in particular. Firms from Australia and New Zealand are expanding their role in Asia. Israelis offer their services wherever they are politically acceptable. Japan's exporting prowess is second to none, and their (frequently not independent) engineers and other technical experts are involved in projects throughout the world.

In Latin America, Colombian consultants, who have performed a great deal of work in the region, will soon be strong competitors in other parts of the world. Brazilian and Mexican consultants are already active in neighboring countries. Costa Rican and Uruguayan professionals also provide consulting services, and many have emigrated with their families to countries where their skills are routinely in demand.

Fishing Where the Fish Are

Our regional summaries suggest that the market for international consultants has contracted and will continue to do so. Competition will be intense among the many firms that proliferated during the fat years of the recent past. Reorganizations, mergers, and failures are inevitable.

Which firms will survive and prosper? From my own experience I can draw three conclusions about international markets:

1. Colonies, trust territories and small countries in the shadow of large developed nations will continue to give preference to consultants of their rulers, protectors, and important neighbors.
2. Newly independent and relatively inexperienced nations count on the continued support of their former rulers and protectors, and frequently choose consultant's from the same traditional sources.
3. Fully independent states, new and old, seek the best consultants they can obtain, often at the lowest possible cost, taking into consideration professional qualifications, commonality in culture, background, religion, and financial advantages.

Government Support for the Home Team

In the international marketplace, it is not unusual to find foreign consultants working hand in hand with their respective governments. France, for example, having a proprietary interest in a number of consulting firms and manufacturing industries, openly steps into carefully predetermined markets to promote French firms. Through the extension of special credit terms, frequently so aggressive in nature that they are called predatory terms, France exercises a noticeable control over consultants' selections and assignments. The United Kingdom has been known to support British consultants all the way from introductions through recommendations, financing and, if that is not enough, by applying diplomatic pressure for contract awards. Spain maintains bilateral agreements with a number of friendly nations, particularly in Latin America, which obliges consultant services to be procured from Spain in return for development grants and/or credits. Canada's financing usually limits the use of consultants strictly to Canadian firms and individuals. Israel, Portugal and New Zealand follow similar policies.

It is interesting to note that governments have started to comprehend the importance of having their nationals engaged as international consultants overseas. A clear understanding has been reached in many countries that if one of their nationals becomes involved in the early stages of a large international project, fellow countrymen will have the best opportunities to benefit from the follow-up activities, such as the delivery of materials, goods, equipment, and services. In realizing this fact, more and more governments are quietly supporting and strengthening their international consultants to make their nationals competitive in the international marketplace. In addition to using official sources to gather commercial and technical intelligence, government-to-government missions, commercial and economic attachés and sometimes even ranking members of the diplomatic foreign service can be found promoting new consulting business activities. And if this were not enough, indirect sales tools have been developed and are being used, such as export incentives, tax rebates, performance guarantees, full insurance at low premium costs, etc. Since the cost of consulting services is important to the client and frequently becomes a decisive factor in the final decision and award of the contract, government support can considerably influence a consulting firm's overhead and net income after taxes and thereby determine its competitiveness. Governments, therefore, have become major competitive elements in the international marketplace.

Conclusion

The world's markets and overseas competition represent opportunities and challenges of enormous proportions. Sovereign governments, powerful international financiers, nationals from many countries, and some of the world's most renowned professionals compete against each other. There exist no uniform rules for the selection of consultants such as the International Federation of Consulting Engineers (FIDIC) has promoted in its recent publication, *Selection by Ability.*

There is no question that there is more work to be done in the international marketplace than all the currently established consultants could handle. But it is just as clear that only a fraction of all these projects will materialize in the foreseeable future and that, therefore, only a relatively small number of international consultants will find new work and professional engagements. These successful consultants will undoubtedly have to be the best prepared, most aggressive, and the most effectively supported by their own governments.

For the convenience of the reader, Appendix A is a listing of the sovereign nations of the world with information about their capital cities, official languages, and dates of independence.

2

SPOTTING AND PURSUING FOREIGN PROSPECTS

How does one learn where the new jobs are? There is no simple answer. There are a great many sources of professional, industrial, institutional, and commercial data to help consultants interested in overseas work. Some are free of charge, others are available at a surprisingly low cost, while a few are prohibitively expensive.

Consultants who succeed in finding new business must be familiar with many areas of marketing. First, of course, is pure and simple technical competence, followed by general professional proficiency, knowledge of international business procedures and trends, international affairs in general, and finally an understanding of conditions in the particular sector at which the consultant aims. The consultant's business is to have knowledge of what serves the client's specific needs. How to market this expertise is the question.

Keeping Informed

The wise consultant reads, and reads thoroughly, in a wide range of publications. These should include:

- Appropriate technical journals
- Relevant professional-society and trade journals
- Special publications and reports of national and international institutions and organizations

- At least one national newspaper of international stature plus a newsweekly
- Foreign (even if these must be English-language editions) newspapers and newsweeklies
- At least one business-news journal

The following are a few samples:

Consulting Specifying Engineer (formerly *Consulting Engineer;* a monthly Technical Publishing magazine)

Finance & Development (a quarterly publication of the International Monetary Fund and the World Bank)

ENR (formerly *Engineering News Record;* a weekly McGraw-Hill publication)

EPRI Journal (published nine times each year by the Electric Power Research Institute)

Financier (a monthly journal of Private Sector Policy)

Interview (a quarterly FIDIC publication)

The Arbitration Journal (a monthly dispute resolution magazine from the American Arbitration Association) Free of charge to members of the AAA

World Bank (and Regional Bank) *Annual Reports*

The World Development Report (an annual publication of the World Bank)

Economic and Social Progress in Latin America (an annual report of the Inter-American Development Bank)

The New York Times

The Wall Street Journal

The Economist

Business Week

Bulletin (Credit Suisse quarterly Swiss Bank magazine) Free of charge

EX-IM News (a weekly report on activities of the Export-Import Bank)

This looks like a lot, and it is time consuming. But these sources are indispensable. Do not treat them as casual reading. Read critically. Analyze what you read. Try to assimilate new data. Always be skeptical and alert to bias in reporting and interpretation. Apply your powers of independent judgment.

Main Sources

Use your membership in professional associations and societies to glean information. In your field, you will find that at least one or two organizations maintain ties with foreign counterparts or belong to an international group. Experienced consultants use these associations as forums for sophisticated shop talk, where beginners can turn to staff and members for guidance. This is occasionally how a novice at international practice is referred to an established firm in need of supplemental or special services. Being known, both to clients and among peers, is part of the professional reputation that follows from, and also invites success, and membership in an international society or association is essential to establishing this recognition.

Large equipment manufacturers and multinational corporations are major agents in the transfer of technology. When they use a consultant's services domestically, they frequently engage them abroad. Consultants, therefore, should keep in touch with domestic industries in their field of expertise, as well as with corresponding industrial or manufacturing associations and business councils.

A new service industry has emerged during the past decade— selling information through conferences, workshops, newsletters, and market analyses. Some of these are well worth the effort and expense; you will find others too general, out of date, even unreliable. Since all consultants need commercial intelligence of some sort, the seminars and newsletters may be a good source, but be critical before you sign up.

Prime sources of both general and specialized information for consultants are the publications of the international development institutions and financing agencies. These detail forthcoming and ongoing projects sponsored by the particular institution, as well as providing other valuable information.

Recommended subscriptions of this type:

Background Notes, U.S. Dept. of State, Bureau of Public Affairs, *Import Bank of the U.S.*

Operational Information on Proposed Projects, Asian Development ment Bank

United Nations Development Business (The Business Edition of Development Forum), includes the Inter-American Development Bank's Monthly Operational Summary

International Business Opportunity Service (IBOS), includes the Technical Data Sheets, The World Bank Monthly Operational Summary, in addition to other related publications on banking and financial activities

Consultants should register with those international organizations that finance or commission projects of interest to them and for which they are qualified. A few agencies automatically place registrants on their mailing list. Once on the list you may receive valuable materials including annual reports, sector papers, statistics, and news releases, and sometimes a direct invitation to submit a proposal. Don't be put off from registering by the long, required forms or cumbersome registration process. This is an indispensable effort that should be made at each institution you believe is significant in your field.

Your firm's general brochures may have an important role in the search for new business, but may not be considered in lieu of a registration form. It will perhaps be accepted as a complement to official documentation, but that is all. Registration at the World Bank, for example, involves the filing of a detailed document (it may come to dozens of pages) that requires extensive research to complete.

In the United States, much useful information can be obtained from the following Washington and New York-based agencies: the International Trade Agency (ITA) of the United States Department of Commerce; the Agency for International Development (AID) of the Department of State; the Export-Import Bank of the United States (EX-IM); the Overseas Private Investment Corporation (OPIC); the Private Funding Export Corporation (PEFCO); and the Foreign Credit Insurance Association (FCIA). Desk officers of the Department of State and Commerce can also help. At the Department of Commerce in Washington is the International Reading Room, an excellent library with helpful staff. Here you can research international markets and, for a nominal charge, obtain material from various U.S. government agencies, other institutions, and the multinational development banks.

The U.S. Department of Commerce also maintains district offices in sixty cities throughout the continental United States, Puerto Rico, Hawaii, and Alaska.

Foreign chambers of commerce and associations, listed in Appendix B, furnish information and can provide introductions.

Similarly, American Chambers of Commerce are active in many countries and will provide information and introductions. Appendix C is a list of their locations.

Promoting New Business

Most overseas engagements result from direct contacts abroad. Nothing is better then being at the right spot at the right time having all the homework done, excellent qualifications on file, and a highly competitive proposal prepared.

Without careful homework, the decisive talk with a prospective client may never come about. Once the consultant has positioned himself in a competitive market, success will be determined by how well he does the detailed work of project identification, client contact, and proposal preparation.

Broad travel is a basic requirement for any international consultant. Much intelligence can be gathered at home. Some contacts can also be made at home and, of course, in the country where the work is to be done. It is often necessary, however, to pursue a project far from its local site, especially when the client and the sources of financing are some distance apart. This frequently happens. For example, if a consultant learns about a sanitation project in Thailand, he may find it productive to visit first with the World Health Organization in Geneva, where the basic study originated, or the Asian Development Bank in Manila, which will provide project financing, and only then with the Thais in Bangkok.

Expertise counts for a great deal in international competition, but so does extensive general knowledge about international work. Prospective clients are often lukewarm when they receive routine introductions to consultants with technical expertise in areas X, Y, and Z. Their interest picks up, however, when a consultant shows he knows something about the client and the client's previous projects. Experience with the kind of project that the client now has in mind and knowledge of the financial requirements for such projects are also impressive.

By the time a newspaper or newsweekly reports new development plans and activities in a distant country, a consultant has probably already performed general advisory services. This is particularly the case for pre-feasibility and pre-investment studies. Before official releases announce loan agreements, special fund transactions, or grant concessions leading to projects financed by the international lending institutions and development agencies, a consultant has usually been involved. That consultant has a good chance to continue with the project, although additional consultants may be needed at later stages. The point is that establishing contacts with prospective clients well in advance of direct work on a project is essential. This requires good local working contacts, extensive reading of newspapers, magazines, and reports, and occasional research.

Foreign governments, by and large, are well aware of the significant role played by international consultants in the creation of infrastructure and other institutional projects. Many countries have established overseas offices through which they inform consultants about proposed developments and forthcoming projects as well as changes in the government agencies which formulate and oversee development plans.

U.S. Embassies and Export Development Offices

The economic and commercial officers of the embassies of the United States are good initial contacts. Virtually all our foreign missions can offer high-quality background information on local political, economic, commercial, and industrial conditions. You will be able to obtain information on local firms, professionals, associations, and agencies, as well as the full names and titles of important functionaries. Introductions to them can be arranged upon request. When an important project is at stake, you may even be able to enlist the official support of the ambassador or the deputy chief of mission.

The United States maintains several export development offices in major cities around the world. A useful service, recently inaugurated by the personnel of these stations, provides secretarial and other assistance to the U.S. traveler at a reasonable cost. Appendix D contains a current list of offices.

Foreign diplomats stationed in Washington may sometimes provide intelligence about projects in their countries, but normally they are not well informed about new business prospects at home. Official country delegations on special missions are another matter. Since they often work closely with the International Monetary Fund and development institutions in Washington and New York, they can be a mine of information.

The more personal contacts you can make, the better. More than once I have benefited from meeting a Minister of a country in

Washington who would have been inaccessible in his own country. One of my earliest engagements in Africa came about through a personal visit with a ranking economics minister who did not have time to see me in his own office, but was most grateful for the small services I was able to do for him while he was delayed in Washington.

It is sometimes best for Mohammed to visit the mountain after it has moved to a more convenient location. It pays to be informed of the travels of foreign officials involved in projects of interest. Be prepared to meet them here rather than in their home countries. Some ranking officials even expect to be met during their overseas travels, and I have often paid courtesy visits away from the host country to consolidate past relationships and facilitate new engagements.

Identifying foreign personal and institutional contacts demands intelligence, information, and, at times, good luck. None of this will help without sound professional qualifications and experience, supplemented by recommendations from satisfied clients, and recognition within your field.

Finally, one way to obtain information is to provide it. Contributing articles to technical journals abroad and delivering lectures or addresses at foreign universities or to professional societies are excellent avenues of promotion.

World Bank and Inter-American Development Bank Offices

The World Bank and the regional development banks maintain local offices in a number of countries. Staffing varies considerably from country to country, but general information is usually available. In some of the emerging nations, World Bank representatives in particular have earned a reputation for great helpfulness to consultants. The international financial institutions and lending agencies will be discussed in detail later.

World Bank and Inter-American Development Bank offices move from time to time. The addresses in Appendices E and F follow are current as of November, 1986.

Other Worthwhile Contacts

Don't forget the importance of social contacts. The Lions, Rotary Clubs, and sports and country clubs are meeting places where you can meet people you might not associate with otherwise. Once in

Bogota, Colombia, I used a tennis club to engineer a meeting with a particularly inaccessible official. (He later became a very good client and trusted friend.) Visits to local universities may lead to an invitation to address students, or a graduating class.

Press conferences, cocktail parties, and sumptuous dinners do little these days to generate business or to enhance a professional reputation. Working breakfasts and lunches, however, are as familiar to clients abroad as they are in the United States.

Bankers throughout the world are, by the nature of their work, well informed and accessible. They tend to be keenly aware of economic and commercial conditions in their regions, and will, to an extent determined by their own interests, freely share this knowledge. Whenever I start to appraise a new market, I visit one or two banks and request a meeting with a ranking officer. Over the years, I have found that local banks usually maintain close ties to government agencies and officials, and can provide access to them. Officers in branches of the large international banks are frequently very sharp observers of the local political and economic scene. A word of caution in dealing with bankers, however: There is no rule of confidentiality between bankers and customers like the one between physicians and their patients, or lawyers and their clients. Information given to a banker might well be passed on to competitors. How much one reveals to a banker is a matter of utmost discretion. On the other hand, once a banking relationship has been established and the importance of confidentialty about professional matters is underscored, there will be less reason for restraint.

Major banks are interconnected and maintain lines of credit throughout the world. A letter of introduction from one banker to another can open many doors. The prospect of holding the account for a large development project can motivate a local bank manager to be very helpful indeed.

Vast reserves of patience, an outgoing personality, and a certain measure of finesse are needed to approach and successfully court a prospective client. The consultant-client relationship certainly cannot be cultivated on a nine-to-five schedule. Moreover, foreign clients are likely to conduct business in ways that reflect their own culture. Consultants must be prepared for cultural differences and adjust to them gracefully.

3

WRITING THE PROPOSAL

Preparing a proposal is a major undertaking that involves writing and editing, translating into one or more foreign languages, printing and binding, and delivering a document in which you put your professional services on the line. A first-class international proposal, with its supporting data and documentation, may cost thousands of dollars—a major investment in the pursuit of new business.

It is well worth the cost and the effort when you have a realistic chance of success. To judge that, you need to ask several questions:

- Does the prospective client really need the services in question? Can he afford them?
- Is the country politically stable and economically sound? Can we afford to work there?
- What has been the experience of foreign consultants in that country? Would we be welcome and receive the cooperation necessary to our work?
- Do we really want this project?
- Can we survive the competition? How qualified and aggressive are our competitors?
- Do we have the staff for such a project? Are they able and willing to work abroad?

A successful electrical supplier once advised members of the august Export Council of New York to blanket the international markets with proposals turned out as fast as possible. This approach was justified, he claimed, by a steady flow of orders amounting to a response of approximately fifteen or twenty percent of the proposals submitted.

Such methods may have worked in the golden age of American exporting, but that era is long past.

A profitable and professionally rewarding international engagement demands management, appropriate expertise, administrative flexibility, and adequate working capital. The preparation of proposals for overseas work must be undertaken selectively and with considerable care.

Proposals are usually prepared in response to an invitation. They may include pre-feasibility and investment studies; preliminary design and cost estimates; definitive design and specification; supervision of construction or construction management; retro-fit and modification; training of host-country nationals; and studies in the areas of education, health, economics, and management. International consultants also often submit unsolicited proposals for professional services. Whatever the impetus for a proposal, most prospective clients will expect the document to contain the following basic parts.

Opening

The first part of any proposal should be a brief letter to the prospective client, referring to the request for proposal or any other motivation for your presentation. It is crucial that you direct this introductory letter to the right party, with correct address and full references. Be careful with the spelling of foreign names and the accepted form of titles and degrees. I know of more than one technically impeccable proposal which was discarded by a foreign government entity simply because of an omitted title or misspelling of a minister's name.

Introducing Yourself

You may not need to introduce your firm to a prospective client with a great deal of detail. If your firm has already been shortlisted, the introduction should be brief and lead quickly to the substance of the proposed work. The introduction may also be brief when a firm is well known to the client through successful work in the area, especially if that reputation is based on projects like the one at hand. But if the proposal represents the first attempt to work in a new country, it is in the consultant's best interest to provide a thorough introduction.

Many consulting firms publish illustrated brochures describing their history and current activities. In some foreign countries, lavish brochures are regarded as mere picture books. Too many firms, small and large, claim to have planned, designed, and built the Brooklyn Bridge, the San Francisco subway system, or the Hoover Dam for the literature of self-promotion to be accepted at face value.

Those charged with selecting consultants really want to know the size and age of the firm, its ownership, and its activities, particularly those demonstrating its qualifications to do the work in question. Present the firm in general terms first, then detail overseas experience. Do not exaggerate. You cannot be expected to have been involved in projects everywhere in the world or to have performed every kind of service. My experience is that clients prefer a realistic account of the firm's experience. They suspect sweeping statements and inflated accounts of firm members' personal involvement in specific projects. Except for small jobs, consulting requires skill in team management and an ability to adapt to varying circumstances. A reliable staff may seem more attractive than dependence on a few talented individuals.

It may be well advised to include a copy of the relevant pages of the registration form filed with the lending institution expected to be involved in the financing of the project. In other cases, merely noting that the firm has had working experience with these institutions is sufficient.

A good introduction always includes several impressive references, such as important international clients (if possible), prominent domestic or multi-national connections, and at least one bank. Bear in mind that while the First National Bank & Trust Company of Darling, Montana, may be an excellent bank, it makes more sense to provide the name of an international institution such as the Morgan Guaranty Bank of New York or the Bank of America in San Francisco.

Terms of Reference and Scope of Work

Requests for proposals (RFPs) are a very mixed lot. Some are clear and precise. Others are vague, incomplete, even contradictory. A consultant should always carefully analyze the request and make sure terms of reference and scope of work in his proposal conform as closely as possible to the client's, yet remain unmistakably the language of the consultant. When proposals are reviewed, those which merely restate the RFP will fare poorly compared to those that meet the request and also reveal professional independence and experience.

Terms of reference and the scope of work are bound to be primary subjects of the negotiations following acceptance of a proposal. To make sure that process goes smoothly, the consultant should go into as much detail as he can regarding these two crucial matters. A consultant may also have good reasons to question the schedule suggested by the client. This must be made clear from the start. Any deviation in the consultant's interpretation of a proposal from the client's wording in the RFP should be explained. Consultants can protect themselves by stipulating that the final terms of reference and the scope of work are subject to mutual agreement to be reached during negotiation of the contract. Your original proposal might be appended to the contract concluded. If a dispute arises, the fact that you documented your qualification at the outset may be instrumental in resolving any misunderstanding on the part of the client.

Schedules

Your client will probably have determined his own schedule for the project and will state a completion date that suits his purposes. Again, as in the case of the terms of reference and the scope of work, a consultant should analyze the schedule and decide if it is professionally feasible. Can the firm comply? Don't fail to consider factors beyond your control: dry and rainy seasons in the tropics; religious and other holidays in certain areas; the number of people and entities participating in or required to review the project. Matters of logistics—obtaining visas and work permits for personnel, import licenses for equipment, and local transport from port of entry to the job site—are minor elements of scheduling that can easily become major complications.

In Guatemala, members of the national highway department once told me how they recognized the truly experienced candidates in a group of unknown consulting firms. They simply looked at the schedules submitted for a feasibility study of a highway several hundred miles from the coast in the rain forests of the Peten Region. The firm that knew what it was up to (and what it was up against) took into account questions of jungle clearing during the dry season; mobilization of river transportation at the end of the rainy season; and, most important, access to the job site through a neighboring country.

Establishing a schedule is a technical and diplomatic balancing act. Consultants will make their own schedules and clients impose theirs, while the reality of an individual project inevitably dictates the compromises with which all parties will have to live.

International engagements do not generally start up as promptly as domestic ones. As an elementary precaution, incorporate every foreseeable delay or potentially delaying difficulty into the schedule of the original proposal. This establishes a time account to draw against as unforeseen circumstances emerge. Instead of following the domestic practice of scheduling straight calendar time for overseas work, use bar graphs to show the various stages and completion dates in days, weeks, or months after start-up. For work likely to be affected by seasonal weather or supply problems, it may be necessary to work out alternate schedules.

Time is always important to every client. Proposals are seldom judged solely on the basis of schedules; but an accommodating, yet realistic, schedule is a strong point that may be of competitive advantage.

It has been my experience that the willingness to waive certain conditions that can delay mobilization may gain the consultant further advantage. If, for example, the reputation and the credit of the client are impeccable, a consultant might agree to mobilize as soon as the agreement is signed, or acknowledged by an official letter to proceed. The start-up could occur prior to the receipt of an irrevocable and confirmed letter of credit. These payment documents require processing time, particularly if international financiers are third parties. Similarly, if agreements and contracts are subject to review or approval, and the consultant is willing to assume the risk that the conditions will not be questioned, he can offer to proceed ahead of schedule. Such gestures will win points, and sometimes even tip the balance in the direction of the consultant prepared to make them.

Doing the Work

Requests for proposals do not state how the work should be performed. That is the consultant's job. Performance is the center of all proposals and this is where the consultant's competence will be put to the test. Is the job to be done in the host country or at the consultant's home office? What steps are proposed, and in what order? How much support will be requested from the client? How independent does the consultant intend to remain? What standards will be followed? Will reports be submitted in more than one language? In metric measurements? Will specifications be issued for international bidding according to the rules and regulations of any particular financial institution or development agency? These and many other conditions should complement the schedule and the scope of work. Finally the proposal should discuss associations, joint ventures, partnerships, and subcontracts.

Associations, Subcontracts, and Joint Ventures

Chapter 8 deals fully with subcontracts, associations and joint ventures. In a proposal, a consultant should explain his experience and policies in these matters. Many countries demand that their nationals participate in all engineering and construction projects. Compliance can be incorporated in the proposal document in the form of a letter of agreement with a local firm or individual detailing the specific services to be rendered. The client will then know that the requirement set forth in the RFP is clearly understood and will be followed. It may, of course, be necessary to include the past history and experience of the local firm or individual in question, as well as appropriate references.

Because time is short in preparing proposals, the selection of qualified local partners can be difficult. If you have worked in the area, or have reliable connections there, this may not present a serious obstacle. But to newcomers, finding local partners can become a sticking point. One way to handle the shortage of time is to write a clause into the proposal that local associates, as required, will be selected either prior to the commencement of negotiations or following notification of the acceptance of the proposal. I have even succeeded in convincing clients to allow the selection of host-country employees or associates after the conclusion of a contract (subject to their approval). This arrangement gave me the benefit of the client's knowledge of qualified local professionals.

A final note on requirements for local involvement: at some point in the course of an international consultant's career, a client, for personal or political reasons, will attempt to control the choice of local partners. The consultant may be constrained to choose between the high road of professional integrity and the low road of accepting what might be a grossly unethical situation. The cost of either choice can be excruciatingly high, just as it is in domestic practice, and the question must therefore be treated by a firm's principals with utmost caution. The course most to be preferred is diplomatically to convince the client that the technical requirements of the project must take precedence, and that local personnel recommended by the client must meet professional and ethical standards.

Staffing

When consulting proposals are evaluated, particularly by competent selection committees in the large development agencies, the qualifications of the project manager and field personnel are given the most serious consideration. The project manager, the individual directly in charge and responsible for the execution of the assignment, need not be the president of the company, the executive vice president of the international division, or the general representative of the company who deals with contracts. Experienced consultants routinely assign their best people to manage international projects. But preparing a proposal, waiting for it to be evaluated and accepted, conducting the ensuing contract negotiations, and finally meeting the conditions upon which start-up is contingent take a great deal of time. By the time the project is actually in need of a manager, the individual originally designated may have been stationed elsewhere, left the firm, or even retired.

You can resolve the problem by including biographies of several project managers in the proposal, with the explanation that one of these, or another person with equivalent qualifications, will be assigned the position, subject to the client's approval, at the time of mobilization. If the client's RFP specifically requires the designation of particular individuals for certain positions, the consultant should comply, but make sure the validity of the proposed assignments is limited to a definite period. The client can tactfully be told that the demands of international work make it impossible to make open-ended commitments for such individuals.

The biographies of a project manager and field personnel will draw close examination and must be prepared carefully. In my experience, staffing of a project is most often the chief factor in a proposal's success or failure. Don't forget that first-rate field performance requires first-rate support from the home office. You don't have to mention everyone in your firm who may become involved in a project, but do include resumes for the principal members of the home office who will be working on it.

Visual Aids

In preparing the schedule for large projects, consultants should graph the proposed timing for the execution of the work. They should also provide organizational charts of the structure of the company, its plans for international set-up, and how it proposes to organize for the project. Support these with copies of company-policy memoranda explaining how the firm operates overseas. This material need not be prepared specifically for each proposal, but should be standard equipment in the consultant's business-development kit. (These materials are discussed in chapter five, "Staffing for Multi-national Engagements.")

Compensation

Fees for consultant services abroad are negotiated very much the way they are at home. (The next chapter, "Negotiating the Contracts Overseas," treats in detail fee considerations of proposals.) The correct time to address this critical subject is during the negotiation period following notice from the client that the consultant's proposal has been accepted.

Occasionally, RFPs may include man-hours, pay scales for various categories of personnel, and other information that will enable an experienced client to estimate the consultant's costs. I have no objection to furnishing this information, provided that the terms of reference and the scope of work are explicit enough for reasonable calculations of man-hour involvement. Inexperienced clients who request cost information but provide incomplete terms of reference and scope of work should be told that fees are determined according to the required number of man-hours, expenses, the firm's overhead, and a reasonable profit. Point out that these can only be established during the process of contract negotiation.

Neither the client's nor the consultant's purposes are served by volunteering compensation, fees, and other cost figures in a proposal. The cost of professional services is determined primarily by salary costs based on compensation according to experience, education and time expenditures, and by overhead costs. These are best explained during negotiations, not in the bidding process, where ability could easily be overshadowed by low-bid consideration. The statement that full disclosure of all costs will be made during negotiations, and that the consulting firm maintains books and records in accordance with established procedures and is willing to submit these to audit, may work to the advantage of the proposal.

Draft Contracts

In recent years, many RFPs have required proposals to include a draft contract. This is a reasonable demand. The draft contract may be in the form of an agreement incorporating the main outline of the proposal, but leaving open matters (for example, parts of the terms of reference, scope of work, scheduling, compensation, and special conditions) which can only be concluded during negotiations. It should be clearly understood that a draft contract is not a binding document, but simply a proposal stating the consultant's normal overseas policies and conditions. You may want to explain in some detail which conditions are subject to special negotiation. The International Federation of Consulting Engineers (FIDIC) has published several excellent model contracts for the use of consulting services. The World Bank is currently in the process of developing its own guidelines for consultants' agreements with its borrowers.

Language

I am often asked whether a proposal should be prepared in the language of the client or that of the consultant. The answer is both. It seems to me that a client is entitled to read about his own project in his own language. If there is to be only one official language for a project, I believe that it should be that of the client.

A clear, technically competent, and well written or translated foreign language proposal goes far to establish language proficiency. But language proficiency will also be on the line when the consultant finally meets personally with the client.

When a host-country client and a third-country international financial agency are involved, proposals may be subject to review and acceptance by both. In that case, more than one language may be necessary for a successful submission. Unless the proposal document is exceptionally long, I recommend that translations appear on opposite pages rather than in separate binders or books. It is easier to work with multiple languages when they are combined in the same volume. This also helps to avoid omissions or mistranslations. The preparation of proposal documents in foreign languages will probably require the use of translation facilities and presses outside the consultant's normal area of operations. International firms maintain current files on technical and commercial translators and printers in areas where they work.

One cautionary word about translations: French spoken by a Canadian citizen from Montreal is not the same French spoken and understood in the Republic of Haiti. Their written French, however, is virtually identical. Spanish spoken by a Cuban is easily understood in Colombia and in Chile, but the Cuban's written Spanish will be rejected by a Colombian as erratic, and by a Chilean as difficult to understand. Many more examples could be cited.

One of the client's first impressions of the consultant's professionalism may be the quality of translation of the proposal. In addition, the accuracy of translation of all subsequent agreements and documents is commensurate with the smooth unfolding of any project. The selection of translators is of crucial importance. Translations for professional services should be made by professional technical translators, not by language professors, and especially not by foreign students seeking extra income, unless they are also professionally and technically qualified.

Style

An Indonesian government official once complained to me that in response to an RFP he had received a dozen volumes from as many consultants, each containing nearly 100 pages, including glossy photos. What he wanted was a to-the-point presentation of some twenty pages accompanied by a copy of a registration form for the World Bank. At about the same time, a minister of public works in Peru was indignant about one foreign consultant who had dared to submit a mere twenty-page proposal for professional services, while everyone else had prepared handsome, bound books with the minister's name printed in gold on the cover. So much for a uniform rule guiding the preparation of proposals! If the decision to award a contract rests solely with one individual, it may be wise, if distasteful, to be as ingratiating as you can (while keeping within the bounds of professional ethics). In the majority of cases, however, it is best to prepare a no-nonsense, strictly professional document, similar in form and content to all other domestic and foreign proposals.

A proposal may include examples of work the firm has performed in other countries. But it must be remembered that enmity between nations can interfere with the neutrality of professional practice. Consultants must know on which side of the many fences of world politics their prospective clients lie, and take care not to impale themselves climbing from one side to another. A reference to an industrial feasibility report for an Israeli project in a proposal for similar work in Libya would be utterly counterproductive. Moreover, foreign clients frequently insist upon confidentiality. The best advice here is to be very judicious.

Field Visits and Presentation

I firmly believe that, prior to the opening of the proposals by the client, consultants should make a personal appearance in the host country. Such visits are usually dictated in any event by the need to gather information about the project and to become familiar with local conditions. Sometimes, when local translation and printing schedules can be coordinated, it may be possible to visit the host country shortly before the time of the proposal presentation. An extended personal visit demonstrates the seriousness of the firm. After a firm has spent many hours preparing a proposal, used expensive translation services, and printed a costly proposal document, the additional thousand dollars or so it would cost to make a personal presentation may be a good investment. If your proposal has been seriously delayed, you may have to submit it personally to the appropriate official. For the most part, however, registered air mail or courier-service delivery—either directly to the client or through the intermediary of an associate or representative—will be satisfactory.

In some countries, professional services proposals are received, as are bids from contractors, by an official of the relevant public authority who simply issues a written receipt. Obviously, a personal presentation here would be a waste of time. Elsewhere it may be required that the document be received by a certain date and time at a certain ministry, addressed to a specific official. In this case, it may be worthwhile to make the personal connection.

When a proposal is directed to a private organization rather than a government or governmental agency, it is fairly easy to judge whether it should be delivered personally, by mail, or through a third party. Keep in mind that whenever an official entity is involved, the review time for the proposal will be considerably longer than for one submitted to a private concern.

4

NEGOTIATING THE CONTRACT OVERSEAS

The good news has arrived: a client wants to negotiate a contract. Your proposal has won against the competition. One hurdle has been jumped. Now comes the hard work of negotiating a contract, for, without a written instrument legally binding upon both client and consultant, the work cannot be done.

The contract sets forth the purposes, responsibilities, conditions, and procedures that will govern the relationship of client and consultant in a project. It must accomodate their respective interests, as well as those of possible third parties such as international-development and financial institutions. These entities are not direct parties to the contract, but their relationship to the client or the consultant may entitle or even require them to assent to it.

This was not always the case. Once, before World War II, I was shown some banana plantations by a prospective client, the United Fruit Company of Honduras. I then received a letter commissioning me to specify and design "adequate irrigation." The same letter, in two sentences, set my fee and the time of delivery. The entire document was one short typewritten page.

Such brevity would not be possible today. Even simple projects entail sophisticated contracting procedures. Contracts for large-scale undertakings inevitably must deal with questions of complex financing, multinational and multiprofessional staffing, and the long-term obligation needed for such international development work. This kind of contract often calls for the expertise of legal specialists, contract administrators, and professional negotiators.

Doing Your Homework

Negotiating a consulting contract is an art for which there are no simple rules, and negotiating in a foreign country involves a form of bargaining which is alien to many American and European professionals. But negotiating has become a vital part of the practice of consulting.

Large international consulting firms often send out a negotiating team. It may include the writer of the original proposal, an accountant or financial expert, the proposed project manager, and an attorney, as well as a corporate officer. Firms without much experience in protracted sessions overseas should seriously consider engaging a negotiator. Specialists are available for such short-term assignments, particularly older, individual consultants who have spent a lifetime in the international arena.

Even after more than three decades of international work, I sometimes run into questions during contract negotiations which I cannot answer without additional information. I do not hesitate to admit this to my clients, for the pretense of knowledge is ruinous, but knowing how to obtain and interpret new information is the mark of a competent consultant.

Professional services are not commodities. The contracts that formalize agreements to buy and sell these services cannot be pulled out of a drawer. Still, some of the model forms of agreement for international consulting services developed over the years by a number of institutions and professional societies can be very useful. Whenever possible, I use the documents published by the International Federation of Consulting Engineers (FIDIC, P.O. Box 86, CH-1000 Lausanne 12, Chailly, Switzerland) as a base for starting negotiations. While some of the material may not apply to a particular case, the framework, overall phrasing, and range of specific considerations provided usually save time and avoid possible errors and omissions.

I find that preparing for a negotiation often consumes more time than the process itself. Most of the preparatory work involves four specific areas:

- scope of work
- general conditions
- compensation
- special conditions

Scope of Work

It is imperative that both client and consultant have an exact understanding of what the work is and of who does what. This agreement must be spelled out in extensive detail in the contract. The scope of work specifies what the consultant produces and provides. It establishes the work plan, schedules, and the choice of personnel. Finally, it is the basis for fees.

General Conditions

General conditions cover important ground. Will the work be done in-house or will parts of it be subcontracted? What are the requirements for progress reports and for administration, both at home and abroad. What is the agreed schedule? What are the provisions for termination of the contract, either by the client or the consultant, before completion of the project? What constitutes force majeure? How are disputes to be resolved? Can the contract be assigned to a third party? Does the contract recognize proprietary rights to processes or studies, designs, and specifications? Does the contract define and direct transfer of know-how? These are only some of the questions which must be addressed as you prepare for a contract negotiation.

Compensation

The question of fees and conditions of payment is probably the most complicated. It is essential in contract negotiation that the derivation of fees be clearly understood. A client is entitled to a clear presentation of the way in which a fee has been estimated. A client who understands how the fee was established will not feel that a consultant's costs or charges are exorbitant. By the same taken, the consultant who carefully formulates the scope of work will not underestimate his fees. He will also be well able to justify his position during negotiation. This rule applies whatever the nature of payment, whether lump-sum, time-charge, direct salary plus a percentage, or percentage of construction cost.

As all aspects of consulting are complicated by the move abroad, so also is the calculation of fees. Many things must be considered when planning an international project. Each of the following items will require detailed calculation.

Direct Time Costs

First is the estimate of direct time cost for all personnel involved in the execution of the work, including the consultant's overseas staff; his home office staff; temporary employees in the host country; and possible temporary staff, including expatriates, local professionals and technicians, or third-country nationals. The negotiating team should be prepared to fully document time-cost figures.

Direct Expense Cost

This covers transportation of personnel from the home office to the job site and any other locations which may be involved; per diems en route; housing and living expenses of staff and their families while away from home; rental of office space and living quarters as required; acquisition of equipment and furniture; and extra costs in preparing personnel to travel, including medical expenses, passports, and visas.

Overhead

There is no established rule for estimating this cost. Some companies maintain one accounting system which includes domestic and international work. Their overhead is calculated on one basis. Other firms differentiate work in the United States and overseas. This produces two distinct overheads, and perhaps more if they maintain separate records and accounting procedures in countries overseas. Overhead is almost always a target of the client's negotiators. The consultant must arrive at the negotiating table well prepared to explain and justify the overhead he proposes with such specific material as certified financial statements and documentation of established company policies.

Subcontracts and Outside Services

In the event work is let to third parties, the consultant should not fail to calculate a reasonable overhead mark-up, since these arrangements require administration and frequently incur the same professional liability as in-house services.

Local Costs

Unless people working out of the home office have up-to-the-minute knowledge and experience of local conditions, it is difficult to anticipate such varied local costs as translations, legal counsel, import duties, taxes, professional registration, drivers, and guards. These are items best figured on the scene. The client may be able to furnish certain services, such as local transportation or security, thus relieving the consultant of some costs, or be able to obtain exemptions from duties and taxes. These possibilities should be explored in preparing for contract negotiation.

Escalation of Costs and Inflation

International engagements often are long. An engineering project may call for staged initial work, such as preinvestment studies; feasibility studies and preliminary design; final design and specifications and supervision of construction. Each phase may involve lengthy examination by the client. If international financial institutions and development agencies are involved, another level of review is likely. You must consider the possible length of time a contract may run and anticipate increases in expenses that may arise from year to year. These should be the subject of specific provisions in the contract language, in addition to appropriate inflation clauses and reasonable exchange rate protection. Political and economic risk analysis is essential to the preparation of a contract defining international relationships.

Contingency

The difficulty of estimating costs for work abroad makes the inclusion of a basic contingency factor in pre-contract calculations a wise move. This is particularly the case for lump-sum contracts.

Profit

Finally, the consulting firm will have to establish a reasonable level of profit. More often than not, this is a percentage added to the total of costs. There has been much debate over the years as to what this should be. I know of no hard and fast rule that can be applied. I recommend that, according to the complexity of the engagement, the profit be closely held to the range used for similar domestic projects.

Special Conditions

No two engineering engagements are alike and rarely, if ever, can two contracts be safely written with identical conditions. Special conditions apply particularly to circumstances likely to influence the execution of the work and affect the consultant's costs. An example is the requirement in some countries that a consulting engineer register as a practicing professional. This can be a costly and time-consuming procedure. If the contracting party is legally empowered to waive registration for its consultants, this should be clearly stated in the agreement. Import restrictions can seriously delay the start-up of work and impede the normal operation of a firm that is accustomed to supplying its personnel with modern instruments, equipment, and vehicles. Customs duties, levied by most governments on all imports, can amount to daunting figures. Exemptions, wherever these are possible, should be detailed under the special conditions. The same advice applies to corporate income taxes, personal income taxes, and any other dues and contributions which are not normally included under direct costs.

In a number of foreign countries, the cost of housing and transportation is extremely high. I know of several nations in which housing is simply unavailable without a one or two-year contract for which the full amount of the rental is paid in advance. An imported vehicle may cost ten times more than its original price at the point of shipment. If the client recognizes these factors and agrees to provide housing and transportation services in order to reduce the contract cost, that agreement should be explicit in the contract under the special conditions clauses.

The working relationship between the client and the consultant and his personnel is fundamental. Character and personality are important. Some consultants will fit into a client's project from the beginning, some will have to "work in," and there are instances of total incompatibility, where removal of the offending individual is the only recourse. This sort of thing also occurs at home, where it is every bit as much a consultant's management headache; but such difficulties are only exacerbated when an individual and his or her family are located half-way around the world. I always write a clause into service contracts stating that the consultant agrees to replace an employee "without cause" at the request of the client, but that the client bears the cost of the replacement. Where an employee fails in his professional performance, or breaks the law, replacement costs are the responsibility of the consultant.

The contract should specify what facilities the client will provide the consultant. When dealing with sovereign governments or government agencies, for example, it is advisable to have contractual confirmation through a "hold harmless clause" that any claims against the consultant by third parties relating to the performance of the consultant's duties will be fully handled by the client's attorneys at no cost to the consultant.

What You Need to Know Before You Go

Once a consultant's negotiating team has developed a strategy based on the review of the proposed scope of work, the general conditions, compensation, and the special conditions, it is time to move on to the conference table. In years past it was not uncommon for a foreign client to travel to the consultant's home office and negotiate a contract there. Some contracts are still negotiated away from the area of the work in question, particularly when international financial agencies and development institutions are involved. For the most part, however, negotiations take place in the client's country and in his office, which is all to the good. A consultant who has not been in the client's country, where he intends to perform professionally, is well advised to spend enough time there before actual negotiations begin to get a feel for the place. Risk analysis, financial planning, and all other forms of conceptual planning cannot replace the experience of being in the local environment.

Language Proficiency

Knowledge of the client's language is indispensable. In negotiating, each word *must* be fully understood by the negotiating parties. Today, contracts are written in one or two languages. It is customary for the client's language to be declared the ruling one, and this will be written into the agreement. Because so many educated foreigners speak English and so few Americans are fluent in any other language, there is a good chance that contract negotiations will be conducted in English. Still, the ruling language of the contract itself is likely to be that of the client. The result is a high degree of dependence on translation service. Embassies of the local chambers of commerce usually are able to provide a list of individual translators.

Legal Considerations and Tax Implications

As important as the language itself is the need for a comprehensive evaluation of the legal and tax implications of a proposed contract. The legal codes of tax systems are by no means equivalent throughout the world. The way things work in the United States may not be taken as a model for taxation in any other country. Unhappily, in some countries, tax regulations have actually exceeded the complexity of the U.S. code. It is imperative to get advice from a local tax expert. Recommendations can usually be obtained through an embassy, a chamber of commerce or a trusted bank.

Professional Registration

Firms or individuals may be subject to the process of professional registration in some countries. This can be a time-consuming affair, and occasionally an expensive one. You need to be completely informed about registration before negotiations begin.

Financial Profiles and Banking Facilities

It makes sense to contact a local bank of good reputation for a reading on local monetary conditions, convertibility of currency into foreign exchange, rates of interest, and other related financial matters. Bankers are usually reliable sources of information and guidance for a variety of financial and commercial activities. I have avoided many pitfalls by discussing the financial aspects of proposed forthcoming negotiations with bankers. But don't forget that bankers are not bound by their code of ethics to maintain the confidentiality of non-client consultations. Be selective and discreet until a lasting professional relationship has been established.

Getting Ready for Negotiating Sessions

You have considered all the points and worked out a complete negotiating strategy. The time has come at last to sit face to face with the client and reach an agreement about the rendering of professional services. Always try to establish and maintain an atmosphere of mutual confidence and trust. In those countries where lengthy bargaining is an honored business custom, I make it known at the outset that I have all the time that may be needed to conclude the negotiations. Where negotiations are seen mainly as a means to be employed economically, I try to reach as quick and direct a conclusion as possible.

The point is that different parties and circumstances require a variety of negotiating techniques and styles. Negotiation is a human art and a process which can involve deep cultural sensibilities. Some time ago, in the Middle East, I spent the better part of the first two sessions discussing ancient cultures, then current political aspirations and general topics in international finance. Once we eased into the details of the contract, the proceedings required only half the time considered typical in that part of the world. I had a very different experience in a European country, where time is perceived as money even more than in the United States. A complete contract had been formulated prior to my meeting with the client. It was presented at a working breakfast, discussed during the morning, and signed immediately after lunch.

Negotiation requires the skills of a psychologist, a diplomat, and a military strategist, as well as plain common sense. One must be capable of gentle insistence and open compromise, one must know one's own mind and still have to understand the position from which one's negotiating partner works.

Any contract for professional services is a very serious commitment. I cannot underline enough the importance that each and every point of the agreement be discussed and clearly understood by both sides before a contract is signed and sealed.

Powers of Attorney

The process of obtaining a valid power of attorney to negotiate and to sign a contract on behalf of a professional service firm in a foreign country exemplifies the administrative requirements of international work. The document is first drawn up by a consultant's own counsel, then signed by an executive officer, and witnessed by the corporate secretary before a notary public. The notary public's signature and license is certified by the county clerk, whose own authority is confirmed by the secretary of the state in which the firm is incorporated, whose power is in turn attested to by the signature of the Secretary of State of the United States of America, stamped with the great seal of the United States. This is not the end of the story. A foreign consular official must now affirm the signature of the Secretary of State of the United States, whereupon the document becomes valid. At this point, however, the document may still not be usable. Some countries require translations of the entire document down to the printing on the stamps and seals. The translation must be performed by a licensed official. In some cases the power of attorney will have to be filed with a designated office of the government of the country to which it is directed, and this often incurs a time-consuming process of registration, authentication, and approval. The entire cost can vary from $50 to $500, excluding attorney's fees, but the time involved will easily consume several weeks.

Compensation

Discussions about payment for professional services must establish the currency in which it will be rendered. Consultants were formerly paid in the currency of their nationality: U.S. consultants would be paid in U.S. dollars, Italians in lira, and Japanese in yen. This is no longer necessarily the case.

Because of exchange fluctuations, shortages of hard currencies, and special conditions imposed by the International Monetary Fund (IMF) or international lenders, foreign clients typically offer to pay a part of the consultant's fee in local currency and part in foreign exchange, although not necessarily in the currency of the consultant's country. When the international financial institutions and development agencies are funding a project, part of the local (on-shore) expenses are usually covered by the borrower (the host country) in local currency as part of their contribution to the project, while the foreign (off-shore) costs are paid by the lender in the consultant's currency. It is one of the major balancing acts in contract negotiation to accomodate both a client's ability to make sufficient payments in a currency of the consultant's preference and the understandable desire of the consultant not to become committed to excessively complicated or high-risk currency transactions. In general, international consultants will seek to cover their expatriates' salaries, overhead, and profit in guaranteed hard currency foreign exchange, while accepting local currency for local costs and on-shore expenses.

Incidentally, the credit-worthiness of a client, even in the world of sophisticated consulting projects, is something you should never take for granted. In many places, ambitions for development far exceed the funds to sustain them. Even when an international development institution funds a project, the consultant must make sure that the funding is in place or actually committed for the work. It is equally important to make sure that the funding of consulting services is part of the financing. Commercial clients can be researched through banks or the U.S. Department of Commerce. But foreign agencies or authorities and their governments, especially new ones, are not easily assessed. This is where experience and research count. You must weigh history, current international politics and economics, and pick up official and unofficial signals from diplomatic and financial informants. A very fine net must be cast for the information that will help you decide whether it is wise to conduct business with agencies of a certain foreign government. Fortunately, U.S. professional service firms can now obtain a measure of commercial and political risk insurance through the Export-Import Bank of the United States, the Foreign Credit Insurance Association, and the Overseas Private Investment Corporation that is similar to coverage that has been available for many years to their foreign counterparts. These facilities should not be overlooked.

Establishing Conditions of Payment

There are many procedures for payment of services. Only in a few countries (unfortunately very few today) is a simple written agreement and a handshake more valid than the most complicated written document. Sometimes, notes issued by the client and pre-dated in accordance with the terms of a contract can be obtained. They are discountable by the banks and thereby assist the consultant's cash flow. Clients are generally willing to pay mobilization expenses and progress payments. The difficulty is assuring that these payments come through within a reasonable time. Frequently a client authorizes payment, but the banking and government bureaucracy delays the transfer of funds. Although the client has paid, the consultant does not receive his money. While there is no universal remedy for this situation, a few measures can be incorporated, where possible, in the compensation and payment clauses.

Revolving Funds and Letters of Credit

Whenever local funds are concerned, these funds may be deposited by the client into a bank account ahead of the consultant's billing. When the invoice comes through, the money is readily available. This can be done through the creation of a revolving fund or the establishment of a letter of credit in local funds.

Where payment in foreign exchange is concerned, the best and safest way is to obtain an irrevocable and confirmed letter of credit which permits the consulting firm to draw against the client's funds as soon as billings have been properly authorized by the client. It is important that letters of credit in foreign exchange be irrevocable and confirmed. 'Irrevocable' means that they cannot be canceled before the date of expiration; 'confirmed' is banking language to the effect that the foreign exchange has actually been deposited overseas into the account of the bank that handles the transaction. But even with an irrevocable and confirmed letter of credit, a consulting firm's billings that must be certified by the client before the consulting firm can proceed to collect may cause difficulties if the client delays the certification. A recently developed technique permits a firm to collect against a letter of credit from the bank within a reasonable period of time, for example, 30 days after invoices have been presented to the client unless the client protests the billings. This procedure forestalls bureaucratic delays and is strongly recommended for inclusion in the payment clause of high-risk clients. Negotiations with clients whose past record or present situation signals the danger of undue delays in the processing of billings are not easy and require an extra measure of diplomacy.

U.S. Dollars vs. Foreign Currencies

While U.S. consultants have traditionally been accustomed to receiving compensation in U.S. dollars, competitiveness has forced the acceptability of payment in other currencies. I believe it will not be long before the Americans will be as ready as consultants from other nations to accept other foreign currency. The American Consulting Engineers Council conducts international workshops to discuss such matters. At a recent session, a principal of a large firm reported that he had reluctantly agreed to accept a substantial payment for services in a Middle Eastern currency, only to find at the time of collection that the U.S. dollar had so declined in relation to that country's currency that he collected a substantial and totally unexpected bonus. Alas, there are many other cases where that kind of situation has an unfortunate ending. The matter of payments requires expert attention at the negotiating table.

The Art of Negotiating

At the start of a negotiating session, consultants should be at their best—prepared, well informed, and well rested. I feel sorry for the foreign professional who arrives at the negotiation table tired from a long trip and not fully alert because of jet lag. A different climate and a totally alien environment don't help. I strongly recommend that negotiators allow enough time to become acclimatized and rest up before sitting down for lengthy discussions and bargaining sessions. This is important not only for the health of the negotiator, but also for the success of the negotiating process.

The first meeting around the conference table is frequently the most difficult one. Client and consultant maneuver for position. Proposal language is brought out of dusty file cabinets. "These are our standard conditions of contract," say the people sitting opposite you. "We have just concluded agreements with your competitors from another country with none of the special conditions you are proposing," states somebody else. "Look at these costs! There should be no special provision for vacation pay or educational expenses." That is the time to quietly take notes, patiently explore details, make comparisons, and search for inconsistencies and unsubstantiated claims. While the final contract price is important to the parties, the goal at all times should be the quality of the services to be performed. The original request for a proposal (RFP) and the submitted proposal must not be ignored, but all possible venues to reach a mutually satisfactory agreement will have to be explored, and concessions may be necessary from both sides.

I strongly recommend that consultants enter into fee discussions without inflating costs or making unreasonable fee demands. A first cost proposal may well include some options and extras that a client with a limited budget would want to decline, thereby opening the opportunity for price negotiations. American professionals' costs are generally competitive with those of most other industrial nations in the international marketplace. Rate differences between U.S. consultants and those of many developing countries (with the notable exception of Brazil) reflect the high degree of U.S. productivity, state of the art expertise, and hi-tech experience in solutions of professional problems.

Negotiating ideally takes place in a calm and friendly atmosphere. Discussions should be conducted tactfully with mutual respect and consideration. Irritating difficulties in international negotiations are sometimes caused by language difficulties, and these should be settled immediately. If certain roadblocks cannot be overcome in one session, push them back for a day or two, when they might be resolved in a different atmosphere. My experience is that a hard but serious negotiation session establishes a bond of mutual respect between the consultant and his client. This is true domestically as well as in the international marketplace. The only real difference is that overseas a negotiator must be not only expert in his professional field but also an accomplished diplomat.

Successful Conclusions

Personally, I enjoy the challenge of international negotiations. I have been fortunate enough to develop real friendships with some of my clients because of tough negotiating sessions and hard bargaining that led to mutual respect. My basic advice for a successful negotiation is to go in fully prepared, be flexible, be forthright, and, above all, act with complete sincerity and honesty.

One last word about negotiating abroad. No agreement is binding until a contract has been signed. Overseas, a document may have to go through translations into other languages, official ratification by various government agencies, and approval by such third parties as international financing agencies. When dealing with sovereign governments, the official opinion of the attorney general as to the legality of the proceedings and documentation may be necessary, and, following that, confirmation by the Central Bank's Board of Exchange.

Once the negotiator departs, the processing of contract documents invariably slows down and meets unexpected difficulties. I always try to complete a negotiation if I can. A few extra days with the client may help to avoid delays, anguish, and expenses later on.

5

STAFFING FOR MULTINATIONAL ENGAGEMENTS

Staffing for multi-national engagements is a most challenging task for the management of any consulting firm. One of your main concerns is to have reliable people available and willing to go overseas as required. Your general personnel policies should be aimed at developing a pool of talent upon which to draw. Particularly delicate is the selection of a person to go overseas for a specific assignment, be it short or long term. If care has been taken in recruitment and follow-up training procedures, candidates can be found within the company. But small firms must often go into the employment market and search for someone with the right qualifications and experience.

Management

Let us first look at management. An experienced international executive who has had top-level responsibilities overseas will have relatively few difficulties in a similar or superior domestic position. The top executives of many large firms serve abroad at one time or another. On the other hand, a manager with an excellent domestic record may find it difficult to operate in the international arena. Lack of overseas experience can be disastrous. When staffing for an overseas engagement, plan to have at least one ranking permanent member on the firm's management team who is experienced in international work. As a company expands into different parts of the world, top-level management must be available for the direction of multinational operations. In Chapter 7 we examine the role of the various levels of management in the performance of international work. This chapter deals with the internal management tasks of staffing, and we will assume that, among the principals of a firm, at least one executive has solid overseas experience in addition to a record of successful domestic management.

Recruiting

Consulting firms seeking to perform professional services outside their country should establish a policy of recruiting personnel in all categories who are interested in multinational work, even when you are involved mainly in domestic projects. Naturally, this is easier said than done. Nevertheless, it is sound management practice to give preference to applicants who have worked overseas or who are interested in international developments. When specific job openings or vacancies for overseas engagements occur, you will obviously recruit candidates qualified and willing to go abroad.

First-class professionals willing to travel or transfer overseas are hard to find. Increasingly, consulting firms turn to personnel specialists to search for, interview, and recommend the engagement of overseas members. Frequently, the time available to fill a vacancy is short, and extensive advertising and interviewing may be necessary. A newcomer in this field may be surprised at the high number of responses to a recruiting advertisement for overseas work. It will not be long, however, before it becomes obvious that a good many people roam the world hopping from job to job. Many of them may have performed well at one time or another, but quite a few eventually become international adventurers whose services will benefit neither employer nor client. Resumes should be carefully read, references painstakingly checked, degrees and registrations verified. Personal interviews with the candidate, his or her spouse, and, at times, their family are also essential.

The need to get to know as much as possible about the personality, outlook, and family of a prospective overseas employee cannot be sufficiently stressed. Regardless of technical competence, a string of degrees, and an impressive social background, people who are strongly prejudiced, eternally pessimistic, crusaders, loners, or prima donnas simply do not work out. These characteristics may become magnified once the individual is beyond the control of the home office and has to perform in a totally new environment.

Among the international job hoppers, quite a few superbly qualified professionals have become used to the good life in foreign countries, with high pay, bonuses, no direct taxes, domestic servants, commissary rights, and even diplomatic privileges. Working abroad, particularly in the lesser developed countries, has caused once-solid citizens to regard themselves as entitled to an array of privileges. Beware of them!

Many firms now make it a practice to interview the spouse of a candidate as thoroughly as the candidate, and with good reason. A supportive spouse and family are among the greatest assets a candidate may have. A dissatisfied, uncooperative wife can easily become a liability and cause her husband's complete failure on an overseas job. When there are teenage children in the family, it is not out of order to take a look at them. Some youngsters have habits which are not acceptable in certain nations. I will leave it to the reader to conclude what might happen if a fourteen-year old who is unwilling to submit to parental discipline gets into legal trouble in a foreign country.

Most firms have a policy of giving preference for overseas jobs to personnel who have been with the company for some time. This is a wise policy. However, even here, the employee's past domestic record is not a guarantee of similar performance abroad. A careful personal interview should be conducted, including husband and wife and even the family members who would accompany them.

International engagements require personnel ranging from highly specialized professionals to skilled technicians and capable administrators. Position descriptions should be in writing, detailing each opening and defining its authority, responsibility, and function, as well as the organizational role and the performance objectives. Often it is not possible to find the ideal candidate and compromises will have to be made. Remember that requirements for adequate performance vary from country to country. Professional registration, for instance, is a prerequisite for employment as an architect or an engineer in the United States, but an ability to speak the language of the host country may be more important for the successful performance of a job in the Middle East or French-speaking Africa. The technical proficiency in air-conditioning of a mechanical engineer will be of little consequence 10,000 feet above sea level in the South American Andes. Experience with cost-saving devices may not be a great asset in labor-intensive markets.

Most consultants are required to travel extensively. A well-organized firm performing services away from its home office normally establishes procedures and practices covering business travel. Companies with engagements in more than one state, and possibly a number of branch offices, will have guidelines for members away from home. International staffing demands more than this; it requires that expert management initially hire and assign the best-qualified and available employees for overseas work, properly prepare them for the engagement, and, finally, give them continous encouraging support at all times. The successful execution of a foreign engagement depends as much upon the professional expertise of the firm and its members as on its internal organization, administrative competence, and personnel policies.

Employment Manuals

In staffing for multi-national engagements, I recommend writing and following a manual that thoroughly covers policies and procedures. This will avoid the misunderstandings that arise so easily over long distances. The manual should be issued to management as well as to employees. (A typical company policy statement covering housing and furniture is provided later in this chapter.)

Company policy memoranda may also have to be presented to clients during negotiations and for audits in order to prove procedures and justify costs. Detailed, written international personnel manuals, therefore, are of particular important for the orderly conduct of recruiting, employment, personnel relations, and control of costs, as well as client information.

Employment Contracts

For domestic employment, consulting firms rarely enter into formal contractual agreements with their employees. But the staffing of international work calls for clear definitions of basic employment conditions and clearly written employment contracts. The contract should state that the employee accepts an overseas position for a determined time, or an assignment abroad for its duration. The contract should also be worded to fulfill the consultant's obligations to the client regarding the staffing for the work to be performed.

If a company incorporates overseas, maintains foreign task forces or branch offices, and customarily transfers members between domestic offices and international posts, the terms of employment contracts must be legally binding and compatible with the governing laws of the host country where the employee will be stationed. Many countries differ significantly in their coverage of social security, forms of insurance, basic compensation, and tax withholding. An overseas-employee contract incorporating general provisions that define the responsibilities of the employee and the company regarding all such obligations must permit changes to comply with the laws applying in the host country. I also recommend that the employment contract stipulate clearly the procedures to be followed in case of disputes, disagreements, and termination. Finally, it is useful, whenever possible, to provide that the laws of the employer's country of incorporation apply. This will avoid situations where a firm finds it may be served with complaints in a foreign country by a disgruntled employee who thinks that legal action in an overseas jurisdiction will help win his case.

Employment contracts provide security for employer and employee alike, and are also valuable documents in dealing with clients. It often happens that, although a consulting firm has agreed to perform certain work with specific personnel, through no fault of the firm, the designated full-time staff member suddenly is no longer available. A previously-drawn contract helps explain this to a client.

For short-term trips abroad and temporary duty overseas, employment contracts are not necessary, but even here a brief letter of assignment and understanding can be helpful.

Classification of International Staff

This is a most important area and must be clearly understood by a firm and its international staff members. Four generally accepted basic categories define international employment in the consulting world:

1. *Full-Time International Staff (FIS).* An FIS is a citizen or legal resident of the country where his firm is established who is stationed overseas with or without his family for extended periods. Full-time international staff are normally recruited specifically for major international assignments or are transferred on a long-term basis from domestic operations.
2. *Temporary International Staff (TIS).* A TIS is a citizen or a legal resident of the country where his firm is established who is stationed overseas on temporary duty. Temporary international staff may be transferred from domestic operations for periods normally not exceeding 90 days or especially recruited for some particular short-term job.

3. *Third-Country Staff (TCS).* A TCS is a citizen or a legal resident of a country other than the one where the firm is established, although he is employed there. Third-country staff may be stationed overseas with their families for extended periods or be charged, like TIS, with temporary, short-term assignments.
4. *Host-Country Staff (HCS).* An HCS is a citizen or legal resident of the country where an international engagement is being performed. He is usually hired locally and resides permanently in the host country with his family.

Staff Compensation

Salary and Bonus

Base salary, incentive or management bonus, or any other form of compensation for FIS, TIS, and TCS categories should be in line with the firm's general domestic schedules. Employees transferring from one foreign post to another, or back to the home office, should not find themselves faced with a cut-back in basic pay. (Various ways to provide for adequate international compensation are discussed below.)

HCS members are generally placed on a company payroll at a level commensurate with their qualifications and the current local rate for the services they are required to perform. Bonuses are sometimes offered as an incentive for the timely completion of difficult and important tasks.

Length of Tour

Short-term and temporary overseas assignments do not call for extra compensation unless they involve personal hardship such as travel in hazardous areas or particularly severe climates. A reasonable percentage added to the base salary can adequately take care of such cases.

When a TIS is required to travel abroad without interruption for a longer period than the maximum 90 days regarded as short term, the employer may consider permitting his spouse and dependents to join him. Alternatively, time may be added to normal domestic vacations or an incentive/management bonus may be payable upon the member's successful completion of his assignment and return to his home base.

FISs and TCSs are stationed overseas for a stipulated period of time and normally return to their home base for domestic or foreign reassignment. Reassignments should be made only after a reasonable period of rest and recreation.

An HCS's terms of employment should be similar to the domestic policies of a consultant, but must not conflict with customary practices in the host country. In case of conflict, host-country norms would take precedence.

Overseas Differential (OSD)

The OSD is a cash incentive for an international assignment separating an FIC, and sometimes a TCS, from his normal environment for an extended period. The OSD is computed as a percentage of base salary. Its magnitude depends upon prevailing living and working conditions at the post. Overseas differential is generally an accepted part of an employee's compensation package.

Overseas Post Allowance (OPA)

Closely related to overseas differential, although quite different, is the overseas post allowance. The purpose of the OPA is to compensate employees for the relative difference in living costs between an assigned location and the country of residence. Different formulas to calculate overseas post allowances have been developed by the consulting industry and others. In the United States, many firms are adopting State Department formulas which were devised for the U.S. foreign service. U.S. government practices, which not very long ago barely competed with those of private industry, have now become quite generous. Hence many firms follow the State Department's guidelines and regulations instead of going to the trouble of developing their own.

Tax Equalization (TE)

Tax equalization is a complicated matter which requires considerable attention. Years ago, consultants were generally exempt from income taxes overseas and most other local surcharges except import duties. As foreign nations have come to depend on the collection of income taxes, it is only reasonable to expect that foreigners should be taxed for salaries earned by working in that country. In the majority of the developing countries, however, income levels are substantially below those of the industrialized nations and a consulting professional might well be in a much higher (the 60 to 80 percent) tax bracket in the country where he is assigned. A responsible employer must see to it that the payment of these taxes does not represent a financial hardship or penalty. Not only would it be practically impossible to hire and keep employees in certain countries, it would encourage cheating, which no reputable firm could countenance. The basic policy for tax equalization is to assure fair and equitable net compensation regardless of the country in which an employee is assigned.

Once in a while, consulting firms negotiate contracts which provide for tax exemption, and there are a few nations where income taxes in certain brackets lie below those of the industrial countries. For these, the same tax equalization policy should apply. In this case, the firm will benefit. I know consulting companies who concentrate their search for new business in certain low-tax countries where a tax equalization bonus will compensate for the higher tax costs they absorb elsewhere.

The HCSs are subject to taxation by their respective countries, and international consultants need not cover them with any special tax equalization. Firms operating with HCSs, however, should be careful to follow local laws and regulations as to tax withholding, social security payments, and severance pay, as well as Christmas bonuses and additional (local) holidays.

Vacations and Home Leave

Company policy governing vacations is part of the employment package. Vacations for overseas personnel are extremely important as they provide not only well-deserved time off from the daily work routine, but needed periods of rest and recreation. This is absolutely essential, particularly when personnel located halfway around the world work under difficult climatic conditions. For those working in an isolated post, planning and looking forward to official periods of vacation is a great morale booster.

Vacation policy for full-time international staff located overseas is generally divided into two categories. Local vacations, usually of one to two weeks, are taken overseas, with the employer providing the time, and the employee paying the cost of transportation and accommodations. For home leave, or terminal vacations, the company assumes the full expenses of time and travel. I have found that many international consultants allow a minimum of one month of home leave for each year of overseas residence.

In addition to local vacations and home leave, well-organized companies also specify holidays, including major national holidays, which the firm's employees are entitled to observe regardless of where they may be residing. For U.S. firms, these would include New Year's Day, the Fourth of July, and Christmas Day. These are usually in addition to customary host-country holidays. A clear-cut vacation and holiday policy is helpful not only as a matter of procedure, but also when calculating yearly working hours, the cost of man-hours, and overhead when estimating jobs and negotiating contracts.

TISs require no different vacation policy from the customary domestic one, except for special considerations as mentioned above.

HCSs vacations should follow the established industry pattern of the host country. These are frequently prescribed by local labor laws.

Sick Leave

Very important to most employees is the knowledge that, if they are absent from their regular duties because of personal illness, or if there is serious sickness or death in the immediate family, there will be company protection and insurance coverage. While most fringe benefits should equally apply to everyone, provision for sick leave overseas may be a matter demanding special consideration in individual cases. Professionals who have elderly parents, for instance, may be reluctant to accept an overseas assignment unless they are certain they will be permitted to return home in case of need. A man with a large family assigned to isolated field work may look for assurance that in case of serious sickness overseas, his family and he, if necessary, may return to a location with acceptable facilities. In my opinion, overseas sick leave policy should be flexible enough to accommodate different needs and circumstances. A reasonable sick leave policy will pay off in terms of satisfied personnel and effective overseas performance.

Medical Examinations and Insurance

Many employers nowadays require employees to take medical examinations prior to employment and enrollment in the company's health and life insurance plans. When preparing for international assignments, medical examinations become particularly important.

In case of illness, the cost of transportation to and from a job site halfway around the world, not to speak of the loss of time, can seriously interfere with scheduled completion time of important works, and make the difference between profit and loss. Exposure to new climatic conditions, different foods, and a variety of other circumstances can precipitate health changes which might not have otherwise become apparent. There are still many places in the world where diseases are not yet fully under control, and where sickness is prevalent. All international staff, therefore, should have a thorough initial examination and periodic checkups. This applies equally to the employee's spouse and dependents when they travel abroad.

Firms that maintain domestic group insurance policies covering the health and life of employees and their dependents should make sure the protection covers international travel as well as world-wide medical treatment and hospitalization.

From time to time, when staffing key personnel for a particularly difficult and selective assignment, companies should take out special medical risk and life insurance policies. This is certainly not a customary practice, but is well advised in exceptional cases. The beneficiary of such a policy could be someone designated by the employee, by the employer, or by both. The replacement of personnel overseas is a costly business, and appropriate insurance coverage may well turn out to be protection at an affordable premium.

Medical examinations and insurance are of particular significance in the FIS, TIS, and TCS categories. A number of foreign nations with advanced social legislation have requirements for covering their nationals for health care and life insurance with which foreign consultants will have to comply.

HCSs should also be offered reasonable health insurance benefits so that there are no substantial disparities among the various employee categories.

Housing and Furniture

No uniform policy exists for provision of housing and furniture for members and their families stationed overseas. Many U.S. firms follow the well-publicized policies of the U.S. Department of State; others have developed their own housing allowances; and a few improvise according to circumstance.

International staff should be able to live in conditions reasonably equivalent to those at home. In some cases, the post allowance will permit the necessary adjustments. In others, the company may have to provide facilities directly. It is advisable to specify what furniture and appliances the employer provides. Employees will then know in advance what to expect and be able to make suitable arrangements. Most families temporarily residing overseas on an international assignment are very concerned with settling in comfortably and securely in the new environment. However, luxury items, family heirlooms, and costly furnishings are best left at home in storage to avoid damage or loss.

Different policies usually apply for the top management of an international task force. A senior company representative may be expected to do a good deal of entertaining. Also, a single professional going abroad will have different housing and furniture needs from a man who transfers with his wife and children.

The administration of housing and furniture policies requires common sense, tact and skill. For some major engagements overseas, I would recommend that the consulting firm first send executives from the personnel or administrative departments in order to prepare for housing and to provide the basic necessities. This may save time and money in the long run. The advance trip can also be used to recruit overseas staff or establish contact with local associates.

Detailed policies covering shipment of personal belongings, household goods, and furnishings, with limits as to weights or expenses, are helpful in maintaining management control and in keeping up harmonious employee relationships. Once again, I recommend the U.S. State Department's regulations (see Appendix G), which can frequently be used with only minor changes.

Educational Allowance

The purpose of educational allowances is to assist the full-time international staff (FIS) located overseas in meeting educational costs incurred while abroad, which may be substantially higher than those in their home community. Normally, overseas educational allowances are provided for primary and secondary school education (kindergarten through twelfth grade in the United States), but not for college or university students.

Allowances are sometimes authorized for foreign language lessons for employees and their spouses at the beginning of an international assignment. In addition, consulting firms generally permit dependent children of full-time international staff not residing abroad with their parents to travel and visit once a year during vacation time at company expense.

There is no standard policy regarding educational allowances and travel expenses. While the U.S. Department of State's policy is clearly defined, professional consultants in private practice may not be able to afford to follow it completely. Additional costs incurred by the private sector will have to be incorporated in the direct cost of a particular engagement or as overhead in the case of a foreign operation. A consulting firm must remain in competition in the international market place.

Since overseas clients sometimes object to what they regard as the extravagances of foreigners, allowances will have to be allotted realistically as well as equitably. The same is true of many other items discussed above. It is a good practice to periodically review staffing and employment policies, after the start up and development of major engagements.

Salary Guidelines

A U.S. Department of State table detailing salaries for government service (GS ratings) and the three grades of foreign service (FSO, FSR, FSS), effective January 4, 1987, is reproduced in Appendix H, consultants from the United States may find it helpful to refer occasionally to current U.S. government compensation when establishing company salary rates and schedules.

6

FINANCING AN INTERNATIONAL OPERATION

The flow of money sustains any project, whether it be a study or the construction of a tangible object. Money management is a very serious and complicated matter in international operations.

Details of financial management may seem peripheral to a consultant's technical knowledge and performance, but they are basic to the success of every project. Financial planning and management is integral to project planning; it figures seriously in contract negotiation and remains important until final payment is received and all outstanding liabilities, including bonds and guarantees, are liquidated.

Mobilizing for Work Abroad

First you should realize that the cost of mobilizing an overseas job is likely to be high, with funds required for some or all of the following categories:

PERSONNEL REQUIREMENTS

- Physical examinations, shots, medical certificates for employees and dependents
- Passports, visas, and special work permits for employees and dependents

- Storage of household goods; export boxing and moving of personal belongings and household goods for employees and dependents
- Provision of overseas housing
- Membership fees in foreign professional societies and clubs
- Prepayment of tuition of employees and dependents

PURCHASES

- Office and field equipment
- Communications facilities

TRANSPORTATION

- Travel for employees and dependents
- Per diems for employees and dependents
- Shipping and baggage charges for luggage and household belongings of employees and dependents
- Shipping charges and insurance premiums for office supplies, office and field equipment, automobiles, and trucks

MISCELLANEOUS

- Insurance: accident and health; life; special hazards, including fire, earthquakes, and floods; kidnap and political risk
- Rental of office space
- Retainers for representatives, agents and lawyers
- Import duties, tax stamps, or bonds
- Initial deposit into foreign bank accounts

This checklist is certainly not exhaustive, yet it suggests the logistical details required for budgeting the preparation of a foreign assignment.

Physicals are stipulated by many international agencies for all consultants prior to their departure for the work site. A certificate of vaccination is often one of the documents needed for international travel. Even when not required by the client or the host country, preventive health care and routine examinations of employees and their dependents is only sensible, particularly for those individuals or families on prolonged assignment.

Moving is always a chore, but international moves are the most demanding. Individuals and families will have to make choices that cannot be remedied at the local shopping mall. International movers are expensive. Personal vehicles need special preparation for trans-oceanic shipment and, of course, should be fully insured. Large, luxurious vehicles will not be admitted into some countries and, for reasons of economy and maintenance, might not be a wise choice in any case. And it must be remembered that there are countries with left-hand drive.

In most cases, housing is one of the costliest overseas expenses. Throughout the developing nations and in some of the highly indus-trialized ones, apartments and houses that meet U.S. standards are difficult to find and extremely expensive. Landlords everywhere seem to be tough businessmen; rents are demanded well in advance, together with sizeable deposits. It is not unusual that housing can be secured only on a year-in-advance rental basis. For members and their families on prolonged stays, firms occasionally purchase housing. This generally entails a cash transaction, since mortgages are diffi-cult to obtain and rates of interest can be prohibitive.

American schools and other educational facilities abroad fre-quently will not enroll students following the start of classes. This makes early arrangements a necessity. Tuition fees vary in differ-ent countries, although they are usually commensurate with private schools in the United States. In a few locations parents are required to become shareholders of school associations or to purchase school bonds. Sometimes employers take title to the shares or bonds. In any event, as suggested in chapter 5, the cost of education for a consultant's dependents is a required expense usually payable by the employer and not by the employee.

Ordering the supplies, materials, and equipment for an overseas job also takes more effort than an equivalent domestic operation. It may well be necessary to purchase telephones, access lines, telex and telefax machines, computer links, and a variety of radio equip-ment and to apply for locations to operate communication equip-ment. Even where these facilities can be rented, substantial depos-its and installation fees should be expected. Copiers, typewriters, calculators, word processors, and computers that operate on stan-dard U.S. 110v., 60 cycle current cannot be used with 220v., 50 cycle current. Adaptors or converters will be necessary. Ordering special, non-standard equipment involves additional expense and delivery time. Automobiles, station wagons, and trucks will have to conform to the legal requirements of host governments, particu-larly with regard to size, weight, and accessory equipment. This may necessitate placing special factory orders for export. Since these orders are not normally handled by domestic dealers, they become cash rather than credit transactions.

Airplane tickets for personnel and dependents, and funds for per diems of employees and their families in transit—including hotel and food costs for a reasonable time prior to departure and following arrival at the destination—amount to thousands of dollars.

Domestic insurance does not always cover every foreign exposure. Policies will have to be amended for adequate extension to international coverage or new and specialized coverages bought. Premiums are not inexpensive.

Office space is sometimes as difficult to obtain as housing, and long-term leases with high initial deposits and prepayment of rental for a year or two are often required.

The start-up of consulting activities in a foreign country often calls for establishing local working connections at an early date. Commercial representatives can be retained to manage visa applications, import licenses, and registrations. Agents may also be needed to prepare the documentation for customs clearances and to activate driving licenses, resident permits, license plates, and social security registration. Host-country lawyers can be very helpful in expediting final contract and credit documents and providing legal advice in many areas. They will, of course, charge their professional fee plus expenses.

Finally, funds have to be on hand for import duties, tax stamps and other local charges, which can be quite substantial. Where bonds are admitted in lieu of actual duty and tax payments, these have to be secured. As it is often advisable because of separate accounting for local and foreign costs to cover all overseas expenses in foreign currency, local bank accounts should be established early in the mobilization stage. These require deposits in order to become operational.

It should be clear by now that the mobilization phase of an international engagement demands heavy outlays of capital. I recommend that whenever possible, provision be made in service agreements that the front-end costs of the start-up are acknowledged as a priority item for immediate reimbursement.

Foreign Exchange

International work inevitably involves financial transactions in foreign currencies. The developing countries in particular now pay for services in their own currency. The time when billings were made out only in hard currencies, and payments were expected in U.S. dollars, German marks, French francs or English pounds, has long passed. Several factors affect the free flow of monies across national boundaries: shortage of foreign exchange because of unfavorable trade balances; unfavorable rates of exchange; social-political and economic instability; special conventions between sovereign nations and the International Monetary Fund; and loan agreements that provide only off-shore components but not expenses.

In countries whose local currency is not readily convertible into foreign exchange, and where the transfer of significant amounts of local currency outside the country is prohibited, it will be necessary to arrange a two-tier system. This way local expenses are covered in local currency and off-shore expenses and fees are covered by direct payment in the appropriate foreign currency or in a currency that is convertible. This last stipulation would likely require the authorization of a central bank, and obtaining such authorization may present difficult financial and political problems.

The high demand for hard currency in many countries has created unofficial, or black, markets in which one U.S. dollar, officially set, say, at the rate of 1:20, will bring 60 local units. The temptation always exists to exploit such differentials, but disregard of the law is a bad way to conduct business and has no place in professional services.

Since no two governments treat their respective exchange problems alike, there are dozens of different procedures, permits, and licenses with which the international consultant must be familiar before he can attempt successfully to finance a new operation abroad. Ministries of finance and related agencies sometimes provide copies of the law and regulations or general guidelines for currency exchange in their nations. I have found, however, that these materials are often out of date as well as difficult to interpret. Thus I recommend consulting local and resident foreign bankers. This is their business. In the event of an unusually complicated situation, you will have to seek a qualified lawyer, preferably before the onset of serious problems. For general information, the commercial and economic sections of foreign consulates and embassies can also be quite helpful.

When a contract specifies payment in two or more currencies corresponding to individual costs in different countries, it should go without saying that this arrangement must be accommodated by an appropriate accounting system.

Local costs will generally include the following:
- Salaries and bonus for host-country and third-country staff

- Overseas post allowance
- Local vacation and sick-leave pay
- Educational allowance
- Housing
- Office rentals, utilities, local transportation
- Per diems for in-country travel
- Import duties, bonds, taxes, stamp duties,
- Social security and insurance premiums
- Office supplies and local purchases
- Retainers and fees for representatives, agents, lawyers
- Bank charges
- Demobilization costs (return to home base)

Foreign costs normally include the following:
- Salaries and bonus for expatriates
- Home leave (vacation) and sick leave pay
- Overhead, including applicable payroll costs
- International travel and per diems
- Physicals, shots, medical certificates
- Passports, visas, and special permits
- Storage of employees' household goods
- Export boxing and moving of personal belongings
- Office supplies and equipment; boxing and shipment
- Premiums for special insurance coverage
- Banking charges

Except in countries with state-controlled economies, it is usually quite easy to convert hard currency like the U.S. dollar, French franc, British pound, German mark, Japanese yen, or Swiss franc into soft currency. The reverse transaction, however, can be all but impossible. Fluctuations on the international money markets are so unpredictable at times that even a number of respected banks in several industrial countries report sizeable losses from time to time. It is surely unwise for a consultant to assume, in addition to his professional responsibilities, the additional risk of foreign exchange speculations.

For the sake of simplicity, economy, and peace of mind, it makes sense to arrange things so that a consultant can obtain foreign exchange without currency conversion. There are a few basic procedures that serve this purpose:

1. The client provides the consultant with a downpayment in local funds to cover on-shore (local) costs during the mobilization stage.
2. The client sets up a revolving fund in local currency to cover

all the consultant's on-shore billings during the entire period of his engagement.

3. The consultant borrows local exchange and repays as the client honors his billings.

The first case is comparatively simple and straightforward. Mobilization costs in local currency are estimated during contract negotiations and included as "payable upon signature of contract" prior to the start-up of the work. The money is then deposited in a local bank by the client and the consultant draws against it as needed. Some clients will want the advance secured by a bond. Such a bond is a standard matter for banks and insurance companies. In Latin America and the Middle East, resident local individuals and firms sometimes perform this service for their associates and clients. The premiums involved in such bonds are usually reasonable and should be charged against overhead on the job.

Revolving funds (in the second example) serve the convenience of the consultant. The advantage here is that the formalities of deposits, billings and collections are established once at the outset of the working relationship, while money is made throughout the duration of the engagement. In a revolving fund, a minimum bank balance, when reached, automatically triggers a pre-arranged process of re-deposit. The point of this mechanism is to insure that there is never a shortage of local operating funds. Contract negotiation is the time when both client and consultant must analyze the utility and security of this financial device. Once in operation, it requires only minimal continual monitoring. Major points of potential conflict regarding revolving funds include the sum by which the account is to be replenished, and the time allowed between notice of depletion and the client's new deposit. These points can be sticky, particularly in the event of changes in the scope of the work, which almost always have significant budget ramifications.

The third approach is merely an ordinary bank loan. Local circumstances, however, may impose comparatively high rates of interest, unusual demands for security, or limit the amount of money available on short. For a consultant, the most direct avenue to a line of credit with foreign bank is through an introduction by his local client and, if possible, by his own bank or a foreign correspondent bank. Since interest is high in many developing countries, the cost of borrowed money must be included in the consultant's fees. Some local banks will accept an overseas foreign exchange deposit that guarantees a local loan although it is not converted into local currency. Otherwise, arrangements can be made through the international correspondents of the local bank. Local branches of foreign

banks established in the host country are often best able to handle
these transactions. As a rule, clients are not, nor do they need to
be, involved in their consultant's choice of banks and credit arrangements. On the other hand, it can be an act of courtesy and good
faith to apprise them of these details, or even solicit their recommendation of the financial institution whose services are to be
retained for the consultant's operations.

To recapitulate one main point: international currency transactions are subject to fluctuations in the relative values of the currencies, and at a given time there may exist or come to be imposed
restrictions on convertibility between soft and hard currencies. These
two factors always remain crucial to any international enterprise.

Increasingly, governments of the developing countries seek to
restrict payment for foreign supplies and services to local currency.
They may even barter local products for goods and services, which
the supplier must then export in order to obtain foreign exchange.
These so-called triangular deals can be quite profitable for international traders who have the facilities and the experience to carry
out international commodities transactions. Export trading companies and certain industries occasionally search for such opportunities. Consultants, however, are for the most part neither financiers nor traders, and should restrain themselves from entering
this highly specialized area. Certainly, the management of international barter is not part of the normal field of competence of a
typical treasurer of a consulting firm.

Letters of Credit

Letters of credit are little known to the domestic service industry,
but widely accepted in international operations. While letters of
credit are primary instruments in international finance, they are
also highly specific agreements created to meet the needs of particular situations. Here, therefore, is a general description of how a
letter of credit operates, not a guide to the detailed form and
conditions to be found in an actual letter of credit.

Irrevocability is a defining feature of a letter of credit. This
simply means that it cannot be revoked during its life time.

When an irrevocable letter of credit is issued in one country for
payment in another, it should also be confirmed. This formality
indicates that the bank which has issued the letter of credit has also
actually transferred the funds to the designated place of payment.

An irrevocable and confirmed letter of credit possesses a lifetime,
known as its validity. This is the period of its operation and may be

set for any length, whether weeks, months, or years. When a letter of credit expires, only the original issuer can extend it, and then the letter of credit must again be for a definite period and with fixed conditions.

Since a letter of credit is by design a financial and contractual mechanism to prevent discrepancies between billing and payment, the conditions it stipulates must be met precisely and without exception. It goes without saying that a letter of credit should be drafted in terms that cannot lead to subsequent disputes among the parties to it.

A simple, irrevocable, and confirmed letter of credit may state that a consultant, upon the submittal of an approved invoice, in conformity with the contract between the consultant and client and not later than a particular date, should be paid a specified amount in a designated currency. The conditions that may obtain in this instance could specify the stationery to be used, the approvals the invoice must display, certification that the work for which the billing is rendered has in fact been completed, and that the amount of the billing conforms both to the contract price and the amount of the letter of credit.

Letters of credit may state approximate amounts instead of specific ones. In financial language, this means that differences of up to plus or minus ten percent are acceptable. Of course, this is not a variation in the terms of the letter of credit, but a variation controlled by terms.

One detail to insure is that the language of the letter of credit be consistent with the contract between consultant and client. Some contracts can be formulated so as to specify a letter of credit, which then makes the letter of credit an administrative detail. It is also important to write the simplest possible conditions for approval of payment, since it does little good to have funds reserved but delayed because of a client's time-consuming procedure for checking invoices. In fact, it is a sensible provision in any contract to limit the time in which a client may approve or reject a billing. It might not be easy to negotiate a ten-day period for the handling of invoices (subject to a formal protest by the client), but it certainly would be well worth the effort. Alternately, a bank could issue payment through the letter of credit procedure, subject to a client's protest within a given period—for example, thirty days.

Letters of credit are comparable to insurance policies in that they must be tailored to the individual needs of each engagement. If properly established and administered, letters of credit not only function as secure channels of payment, but can in fact be used as collateral for loans.

Although letters of credit most frequently are used for the transfer of funds from one country to another, they can also be opened for payment in local currency within the country of operation. Consultants in need of operating capital will find that a letter of credit is highly regarded as a security, and that even when they are unknown to a new bank, a valid letter of credit may help them obtain lower rates of interest and reduced bank charges for local loan applications than would otherwise be possible.

Credit Cards

Plastic, as credit cards are now called, has conquered the free world. There is practically no expense in virtually any part of the globe that major cards will not cover. Visa and MasterCard are the best known; however, the less well known International Air Travel Card is accepted for practically all commercial airline charges. No doubt there are regions removed from the international avenues of commerce and tourism where cash still reigns, but anyone destined for such places is probably astute enough to anticipate the need for hard currency cash.

The buying power of credit cards makes it necessary to dwell on the responsibility conferred in authorizing their use. Who gets one, and with what limits or controls, is an important question each firm must decide for itself. It is much easier now to keep track of these instruments, as computer processing has made it possible for one credit card company to provide spreadsheet accounting for the use of all the cards issued in the name of one firm.

It should also be noted that credit card charges in foreign currencies are not converted on the date of purchase. Credit card companies perform bulk exchanges timed to yield the most favorable rates. Because of floating exchanges, therefore, the calculation of the cost of a transaction in foreign currency with a credit card is necessarily approximate. On the other hand, the rate of exchange is likely to turn out better than in the case of a cash transaction or one with traveler's checks.

Finally, the users of U.S. dollar credit cards must understand that they will be billed by the credit card companies in U.S. dollars and not in the foreign currencies for which they were originally changed.

Cash Funds

As a general rule, it is wise to travel with as little cash as possible and to keep as little of it on hand as possible. Some money is always needed for things such as gratuities, cab fares, small purchases, and minor emergencies. Credit cards otherwise easily absorb major short-term needs. Traveler's checks, while not inexpensive, are comparatively safe and available in numerous currencies. Traveler's checks, interestingly, are sometimes not convertible where credit cards are accepted. So it is worth the small effort to learn in advance which cash substitutes are preferred in particular foreign countries. Cash itself, of course, is best obtained in local banks. Lines of credit can be established with the assistance of a letter of introduction written by an international bank, which can also arrange for a traveler's letter of credit, an instrument stipulating a sum in one country that is to be received in another. A traveler's letter of credit differs from a line of credit in that it is a fixed, one-sum transaction.

Remember again that a number of countries prohibit the free movement of currencies across their borders. Several socialist countries of Eastern Europe, for example, limit the amount of foreign currency with which an individual may enter, and also proscribe departure with any amount of local money. Other countries will require detailed accounting of currency movement. For most purposes, then, it is best not to carry significant sums of cash across international boundaries, but to arrange for transfers through international banking facilities. Vouchers of all financial transactions, money exchanges, interest charges, and declarations are important documents that should be kept and filed.

Collections

Since international operations are best financed with working capital derived from income, it is necessary at the outset of a project to establish an efficient process for the payment of services and reimbursable expenses. Agreement on billing and collection procedures is an absolutely essential part of the professional relationship between consultant and client. Provisions must be made to ensure the availability of foreign exchange for off-shore payments and local currency for on-shore obligations. Delays in submitting invoices can become extremely costly. Untimely payments are frequently inevitable, and they always cause financial havoc. Foreign clients do not always understand the consequences of delayed payments. A short-fall in receivables makes it necessary for the consultant to borrow money locally in order to cover local salaries and expenses. He will have to pay the local interest rate charged to foreign borrowers. Interest is typically not a budgeted item, and may be hard to recover. There may also be a host of currency conversion problems attached to repayment of the loan. In this case, a five percent penalty clause for late payment would not help much if the interest on the loan is significantly higher, or loan money cannot be obtained in time. In any case, few clients take kindly to such penalty clauses in the contract. The path of wisdom, then, is to formulate a contractual link between payments that are late as defined in the contract, and the consequences caused to the consultant by the lateness. You can negotiate the definition of the amount of late payment necessary to trigger penalty mechanisms. Some compromise will make protective provisions for the consultant more palatable to the client.

A strong word of caution: the foreign governments, resplendent in their sovereignty, who are frequently the clients of international consultants, are not easy customers to muscle when their payments come up short. Perhaps they will be reasonable and indeed honorable. Much history suggests they will not. The great tradition of U.S. advocacy is far less persuasive to a foreign power, or to an institution politically connected with or outrightly protected by one. Prudence in international work requires hard thinking about the kind of leverage a consultant has at his disposal in the event of a dispute or explicit violation of contract. The consultant must also assess the forces that may in turn be brought to bear against him. These risks keep international players on their toes.

Some measure of self-protection can be found in insurance against nonconvertibility of currencies, expropriation, war, and internal revolution that is offered to investors by the Overseas Private Investment Corporation (OPIC). Insurance against commercial risks such as insolvency, substantially delayed payments, and certain political risks is offered by the Foreign Credit Insurance Association (FCIA) in conjunction with the Export-Import Bank of the United States (Ex-Im). These organizations are government-supported agencies designed to assist U.S. overseas trade. Their policies are offered as services to U.S. manufacturers and service professionals working to profit in the world market. In the end, however, the best insurance remains the good judgment by which a player in the international arena enters into a sound contract or avoids unreasonable exposure.

Revolving Funds

Revolving funds, like letters of credit, function by providing a collection facility to be established by the client for the use of the consultant. Revolving funds, however, are a good deal less complicated than letters of credit, since they are unconditional accounts without strict controls or restrictions and generally may be opened as easily as any other account. They are used primarily for local currency transactions. Following draw-down by the consultant, the client simply replenishes the account in anticipation of further collections by the consultant.

The primary safeguard for a client supplying a revolving fund is to stop making deposits. As a further guarantee, the consultant may be requested to provide a bond to cover the revolving-fund transactions. The rates for such bonds are reasonable, especially considering the convenience they afford.

Working With Associates

While associations and joint venture are topics unto themselves (and the subject of a later chapter), it is important to mention obligations to venture partners in connection with financing foreign operations. Joint venture agreements, subcontracts and other forms of association are fields in which discord easily grows. These working relationships must be formalized in appropriate contracts, which in turn are clearly linked to the primary consultant's contractual relationship with the client.

One of the first financial considerations in working with an associate or partner overseas is the incorporation of his cash flow into the financing scheme of the operation. It is reasonable to scale this contribution to the various operating costs in direct proportion to his participation in the responsibility for the project as a whole and the anticipated profit from it. Whatever the actual allocation of fiscal responsibilities, however, it is generally best to present the client with one combined statement that integrates the roles of the project's working members, and makes the distribution of reimbursable expenses and payment of fees to partners, associates, or subcontractors the task of the lead consultant.

Should it be necessary to present a client with separate billings for the services of the primary consultant and a local partner or associate, safeguards and procedures for paying the local member should be similar to those for the principal. Fees and expenses should be contractually defined, and collection procedures and payment schedules contractually specified. Remember that capital and lines of credit for individuals and small firms, especially in the developing countries, are often hard to obtain, so they are particularly vulnerable to cash-flow problems. Your partners should be protected against compromising situations as far as possible.

On the other hand, a local partner whose financial position allows him to advance host-country currency and so ease the foreign consultant's exchange exposure is a precious find. Another rarity is the associate able to assume responsibility for local costs beyond the extent of his participation, or even entirely, in return for a larger share of foreign-exchange income. Tax considerations, personal reasons, or the desire to be free of local currency restrictions may underlie such moves.

There are many possible structures for a group providing professional services. Each form of organization carries financial ramifications. Legal considerations, of course, take precedence in these matters, and it is sound practice to obtain a client's approval of the professional and financial arrangements the consultant proposes to make in the host country.

Conclusion

The management of all professional services projects is both an art and a science. And, of course, all projects entail difficulties and complications. In international work, language, distance, time delays, extended communications (satellite networks notwithstanding), and unfamiliar environments, laws, and practices exacerbate the things that normally go awry. Monitoring and control procedures must compensate for all these.

It is advisable, if not indispensable, that ranking members of a consultant's organization be involved administratively as well as technically in international projects. Corporate officers, treasurers and controllers should attend major contract negotiations for overseas jobs and personally establish financial controls in the field.

Banking, as should be clear now, is a matter for keen attention, on location, at regional headquarters, and in the home office. Good project planning includes learning about banking practices in the area of the project, as well as securing a timely and legally correct designation of powers of attorney for financial transactions. Foreign bank statements should be mailed not only to the local office, but to at least one other administrative center that performs routine oversight duties. Since many overseas banks do not return cancelled checks with their statements, multiple detailed records have to be kept of all drafts. The importance, and burden, of oversight increases with the number of currencies and associates involved in a project.

7

ADMINISTERING OVERSEAS WORK

The execution of international jobs is very different from domestic work in that the need for administrative support places heavy demands on management skills.

Because this book is written for individuals and consulting firms of varying sizes, and also covers a variety of projects all over the world, I can only suggest that specific guidelines be issued and followed when the time comes to administer an international engagement.

From one point of view, domestic consulting work, which demands sophisticated high-tech and labor-saving operations, may be more complicated than foreign work. But even simple overseas projects, when executed according to multiple technical standards, in more than one language, and with multi-national rather than domestic specifications, require extra care and special professional attention. This chapter discusses techniques that have been developed and are followed by international firms to administer efficiently overseas projects.

Management

A principal of a firm, a partner, or a director of the corporation should be designated as the top management representative for the particular international contract. This individual must have the responsibility and authority to direct the consultant's international commitments. In chapter 5, I pointed out the importance of experienced international management. One fully responsible individual must have jurisdiction over all matters, professional and administrative. Ideally, the person with the decision-making powers will be able to keep close enough personal control of foreign operations to make timely decisions and avoid costly mistakes. Things are tough in the domestic field when an error is committed and corrections have to be made. Halfway around the world, poor professional judgment or a slip-up in client relations can not only mean the difference between profit and loss on a particular job, but can endanger a firm's reputation and continued ability to operate overseas.

The Alert Traveler

Depending on the size of the consultant's organization, selected members of management and staff must be prepared to travel on short notice. Passports have to be kept current, visas applied for so as to permit hurried departures, and vaccinations kept up to date. Many experienced international consultants never leave home without carrying valid passports, international health certificates, credit cards, and a reasonable supply of traveler's checks. To give one personal example: while attending a recent meeting in Miami, Florida, I received a call to attend an urgent meeting in Santo Dominigo in the Dominican Republic. The fact that I had my passport with me made it possible to proceed immediately, without having to return home first. Being prepared to move fast pays off in client relations, and also keeps costs down.

Passports and Visas

U.S. passports are valid for ten years and will be issued by the Department of State's Passport Office in Washington, D.C. Applications may be made to clerks of designated state or federal courts. Frequent international travelers should indicate on their passport application that they intend to take many international trips, in which case the passport will contain more pages than the ordinary tourist travel document. If a passport fills up with visa entry and exit stamps, additional pages can be added by U.S. consular officials overseas or State Department passport officers in this country.

For business purposes, it is recommended that passports cover individuals rather than families. This will permit a husband to travel without his wife, and children without their parents. It is easier to handle travel documents for each person than for family groups who may separate at one time or another.

A tourist card sometimes is all that is needed by U.S. citizens visiting foreign countries for short periods of time; visas issued by foreign consular officials are required by others. Work permits are a must almost anywhere when consultants' personnel have to perform professional services over a prolonged period of time in the host country. Never travel without the proper visas and permits. Any omission will certainly cause lost time and possibly local fines and disqualification to work.

When a firm has official engagements in foreign countries, governments sometimes issue service, courtesy, or other types of visas which permit members of the consultant's team to enter and leave the country as required. It is good policy to have these visas ready and prepared for all your staff well ahead of the time of assignment, and even on a stand-by basis.

U.S. citizens should be aware that foreign visas should not exceed the validity dates of the U.S. passport. If they do, difficulties arise because upon issuance of a new passport, the U.S. authorities invalidate the old one. Consequently, U.S. passports may have to be renewed before their actual expiration date.

Overseas Travel

International engagements force consultants to travel frequently. For the international president, vice president of foreign operations, or head of the overseas division, I recommend that trips abroad do not exceed twenty-one working days. Recent surveys conducted in several countries indicate that the traveling executive loses efficiency after three weeks in the field. This also applies to the consultant's staff as well, but it is usually the top men who are required to put in long hours of daytime work, in addition to evening social functions. A good many of my friends, when they travel from country to country, use breakfasts, luncheons and dinners for business meetings. Three weeks of that kind of work take their toll. A quick return to the home office for some time in familiar surroundings permits them to recharge their batteries before going out again.

Much has been said and written lately about time-lag and the effects of international jet travel. There is no doubt that changes from one time zone to another, along with exposure to different climates and altitudes affect the traveler's health, his general disposition, and, probably more often than is recognized, his ability to make sound decisions. Jet travel has different effects on different people; some tire easily, while others claim that they rest better in flight than at home. Personally, particularly during long journeys, I like to settle down and work, as I find few other places where one is less disturbed than on a plane. I do admit that sometimes I am more tired stepping off a plane eight hours after boarding than I would be after leaving my office after putting in eight hours of work.

First Class or Economy?

Most established companies have definite policies setting forth the style in which they expect their personnel to travel and to live. Domestically, many executives are entitled to use first-class transportation with rare exceptions; a number of consultants also permit first-class privileges for long trips exceeding six hours of uninterrupted flights.

International clients and their lenders are generally sensitive about the high expense of first class and sometimes refuse to cover more than the cost of economy class. Some airlines have recently provided business class accommodations at a cost significantly below first class and only slightly higher than economy class. Consultants should be flexible about travel costs, which can be quite substantial. I know of cases of very tall or heavy individuals who simply do not fit into economy-class seats on most planes. Professionals with physical handicaps will also fare better in more spacious seats. On the other hand, experienced world travelers can normally adjust to the seating in economy or business class. Clients frequently stipulate which class their consultants are to use for travel.

Years ago it was prestigious to travel first class, a left-over from the days of trans-Atlantic and Pacific steamers. Today, one meets as many important contacts in the economy section as in first class; in fact, an increasing number of airlines use planes with only one class on domestic and international routes.

Similar considerations should be given to hotels abroad. Many well-known national chains catering to businessmen in the United States have established luxurious facilities overseas aimed principally at the tourist trade. Often these "little Americas" are out of town and require expensive taxi or rental-car transportation for the consultant as he moves about. Centrally located, comfortable, and clean accommodations are important. Find out which foreign cities offer their own perfectly acceptable hotels. As a matter of fact, the foreign business visitor is usually better received and attended there than in the tourist-oriented international hotel, and at considerable savings in rates, transportation, and time.

Beware of Heights

High altitudes, such as in Mexico City; Nairobi, Kenya; Bogota, Colombia; Quito, Ecuador; Addis Ababa, Ethiopia; and LaPaz, Bolivia have a marked effect on travelers. Personnel should be cautioned to move slowly and to avoid excitement upon arrival. One should stay away totally from alcoholic beverages, heavy foods, and even smoking for the first twenty-four hours, at least.

Communications

Very few businessmen need to be convinced nowadays that efficient means of communications, and effective communication policies, should receive top priority. Within the United States, we enjoy excellent telephone systems and our mail service is still reasonably reliable compared to other countries. Communicating internationally, however, poses problems. Telephone systems via satellites, telex, and cable connections are constantly improving, but still far from perfect. International consultants should move quickly and decisively to establish the best available systems of communications within their overseas operations.

Telephones

International telephone service is quite reliable and relatively inexpensive. In a number of countries, however, the installation of a local telephone requires long waiting periods and high subscribers' fees. Also, while it may be easy to telephone several thousand miles across the oceans from one country's capital to another, it may be nearly impossible to obtain a satisfactory local connection. Telephone facilities overseas should be checked out at an early stage of a project. Because of occasional circuit difficulties in this country and overseas, the company should list not only the official office numbers, but the residences of principal expatriate and local employees as well. Communications can thus be maintained outside of normal business hours, if necessary.

International Cables

Cable messages, transmitted internationally via radio or trans-Atlantic cables, can be compared to domestic telegrams. As there is a charge for every word, highly specialized consultants develop their own private cable codes whereby combinations of letters stand for whole sentences or an entire professional operation. The use of coded cables is customary among commodity dealers and international merchants. To a lesser degree, codes can be a cost saving factor for a consultant, as well as an insurance of confidentiality where messages have economic and political implications. Private cable codes, however, are forbidden in a few countries. A consultant must use his judgement (and estimate costs) before deciding if the extensive work needed to prepare codes and train personnel in coding and decoding of messages is worth the trouble.

The international communications companies accept code names in lieu of full, detailed addresses. Registration of a coded address has to be undertaken once a year in each location. In quite a few countries, the cable companies will also accept delivery instructions for code addresses. Messages received after business hours or during holidays, for instance, can be directed to a private residence or transmitted by telephone, pending delivery of the printed cable when the offices next open for business. A full understanding of international cable practices is easy to come by. Representatives of the service companies are available for full explanations, and printed material is readily obtained.

Telex

Telex service is one of the great innovations of our times, and I sometimes wonder how it was possible to work internationally without it. The telex allows for conferences whereby typed messages may go to and fro directly between sender and receiver. Telex can be used for the simple transmittal of messages or for question and answer sessions. As in the case of cable addresses, a consultant should register his firm and have the proper telex equipment installed in his domestic headquarters and overseas task force offices. Sometimes it is not possible to obtain promptly a telex installation overseas. And overseas costs may be excessive for certain short-term engagements. Public booths are being increasingly installed throughout the world, and messages can be sent and conferences can originate there without too much inconvenience. Hotels almost always have telex facilities for their reservation services that they will also make available for guests. One of the earliest steps in establishing overseas communications is to investigate telex facilities and set up procedures to obtain the most trouble-free communications that are available.

Citizenband, VHF, and Radio Transmissions

Where special conditions prevent the use of traditional, public communication systems, consultants may have to devise their own. This is particularly so for local office-to-field operation communications, or when it is necessary to be in touch with mobile units.

The electronics industry has lately developed two-way systems which can work in varying conditions at quite reasonable costs. Special permits and operator licenses may be required, but are usually easily obtainable. Prior information on available frequencies will assure that equipment can be properly set up.

Mail, Air Freight, and Courier Services

The mails have to be watched everywhere, including the industrialized countries. Sometimes the best organized and most reliable mail systems break down because of strikes, political upheaval, labor difficulties, or as a consequence of natural disasters. After the earthquake in Guatemala some years ago, dedicated Guatemalan post-office employees saved most of the mail but had a hard time distributing it. A recent protest by postal workers in Italy so bogged down the mails that uncounted letters, parcels, and packages never reached their destinations. To insure at least that mail is under control as far as the consultant's powers go, international mailings should be numbered in such a way that writers and addressees are able to check and trace remittances. In some instances, originals should be duplicated and sent out twice or more at intervals of one or two days. It behooves a consultant to investigate carefully the various options of service at his disposal, including delivery via airline and, on some official engagements, the use of courier services and diplomatic pouches. International commercial courier services have developed throughout the world during the past decade; for a fairly reasonable cost it is possible now to send mail, reports, and drawings from one country to another within 48 hours or less.

Overseas Office Facilities

In order to do their work properly consultants should have adequate facilities. I certainly do not advocate luxuriously furnished suites with all the newest gadgets, but I do believe in quiet, well-lit, secure, and properly ventilated offices where a person can enjoy spending his working hours. Enlightened management recognizes that good working conditions are conducive to efficiency. The costs involved often are considerable in certain areas overseas, and contract negotiations, as well as a policy decision to establish a branch in a given area, must take these costs into account.

At times, consultants have little choice if a client requests that the expatriates move in with the host-country organization. Because of local associations or joint ventures, the foreign consultant may also be invited to share his local friends' facilities. But it is different when the choice is entirely the foreign consultant's. The selection of functional offices, comfortable furnishings, and modern equipment should be high on the list of priorities when setting up shop overseas.

Consulting engineers are sometimes required to maintain personnel permanently on construction sites far away from civilization. Here it pays to specify at an early date what the client or the contractor is to furnish in the line of office facilities. Self-contained trailers have become increasingly popular. If the installation is more like a camp, it should meet certain minimum standards, particularly when it comes to protecting against prevailing climatic conditions. Sanitary facilities must be good enough to make sure that consultants are not exposed to preventable health risks, and arrangements for the personal safety and security of the consultant's staff should be made well in advance of the start-up of work.

Consultants are frequently able to specify furnishings and equipment on assignment abroad. I recommend that before deciding to import articles, the local market be surveyed. Electrical current should be checked. The United States standard, 110/220 volts, 60 cycles, does not apply in many industrialized nations, and even less in the developing countries. All equipment operating on electricity—including the expatriate's electric shaver and toothbrush, as well as the office copying machine, typewriter, computers, and word processors—will have to be adaptable.

Some company policies specify the brands of machines to be used. This is justified for domestic operations. Overseas, however, an experienced manager will carefully survey the local market with regard to service facilities and availability of parts. The best of the domestic makes, for which unlimited service is available at home, may not last long where the manufacturer's representative is not geared to service his firm's products.

Office security is another factor that should not be overlooked. File cabinets and safes should fully protect valuable documents. An expatriate should never forget that even a simple electronic calculator worth less than twenty-five dollars at home may be the object of a break-in.

Protection against the environment is something else that frequently defeats a newcomer to the field. Heavy humidity during the rainy season can damage and destroy records in very little time, and floods are commonplace in some of the world's lowlands. Civil disturbances, unexpected riots, and even open warfare have been known to interrupt international development work. How well protected are your overseas offices against these eventualities?

Vehicles

Consulting work requires mobility. In setting up foreign operations, making sure that the right vehicles are available when you need them calls for meticulous planning.

The use of automobiles for everyday personal and business use is still a luxury in some countries. Economy-sized American cars are often the largest automobiles permitted in certain developing nations. Large or medium-sized vehicles would be totally impractical, even if they could be imported. To purchase overseas and import or to buy locally is always a tough question. I recommend a car or a fleet of vehicles that can be serviced locally by dealers with trained mechanics and a supply of parts on hand.

When negotiating contracts, clients sometimes offer consultants the use of local vehicles and drivers. In my experience, this is not satisfactory. Too often the automobile you need cannot be made available on time, drivers turn out to have other obligations, and local maintenance is not up to acceptable standards. I strongly recommend that consultants try to maintain full control over their transportation.

To Drive or Not to Drive?

A U.S. driving license is usually valid in a foreign country for a limited time, usually up to 30 days after arrival. Thereafter, it may be necessary to obtain local driving licenses. A number of sovereign nations also recognize the international driving license issued by the American Automobile Association. According to some reports, these licenses are regarded as valid for tourism only, and you should make certain that no expatriate drives unless his license is valid.

Not all domestic insurance automatically extends to coverage in foreign countries. Companies sometimes obtain international coverage for international staff through their U.S. carrier. In case of accidents and claims, however, it may be better to buy local insurance coverage. (It also makes for good local relations.) Insurance company agents overseas usually belong to an influential group of businessmen who will appreciate the opportunity to write policies for foreign consultants, who are considered excellent risks everywhere.

As everybody knows, accidents do happen, even fatal ones. Under Anglo-American law, everybody is innocent until proven guilty. Roman law is quite different. Even in case of a simple accident, you may be considered guilty unless you can prove that you are innocent. In a number of sovereign nations, fatal automobile accidents carry extremely severe punishment, regardless of guilt. I can never forget the case of a most honorable Swiss citizen in a Latin American country, who was blinded at night on a narrow country road by an oncoming car and plowed into a group of men standing by the roadside, killing several of them. He was imprisoned for several months until his case came up for trial, and then condemned to support the victims families for life. He never recovered from this tragic accident. Unable to leave the country to pursue his business activities, he finally committed suicide. A responsible consultant will thoroughly investigate local laws and practices regarding driving automobiles under a variety of circumstances. He may be better off hiring local drivers for his expatriate and third-country employees in order to avoid uninsurable and unreasonable risks.

Insurance Coverage

Consultants working in foreign countries need to consider a variety of risks and insurance that is available to cover them. This goes beyond social security, accident, and health and life insurance to include coverage for property and work-under-progress, damage to third parties, and special local hazards. Kidnapping of company employees, for instance, which was unthinkable until fairly recently, is now one of the dangers we all face. Obviously, insurance against kidnapping is best taken out discreetly in a third country and with the knowledge of only the most limited number of trustworthy insiders. Otherwise, a kidnapping insurance policy would quickly become a hunting license.

Banking Abroad

The previous chapter dealt with domestic and international financing. In order to set up a businesslike foreign operation, host-country banking connections are desirable. These should match as closely as possible the domestic banking arrangements to which the consultant is accustomed. Opening accounts, transfers of funds, payments of drafts and many other routine transactions have to be carefully registered and supervised. Financial controls and banking practices vary from country to country, as do laws regarding international transactions.

Large international banks have foreign branches or maintain relationships overseas through correspondents and representatives. Banking is a competitive business, and bankers look for customers just as consultants search for clients. Information about host-country banking facilities, therefore, is relatively easy to come by, and preliminary arrangements should be completed promptly so that basic operations may proceed efficiently. Hurried last minute arrangements often lead to costly misadventures.

Consultants may also find it beneficial to adjust customary domestic procedures so that the firm operates more efficiently in international markets which follow different practices.

It should be noted that corporate powers of attorney, or resolutions by the partners of a firm or a company's board of directors are required in a number of countries before bank accounts can be established. It may be necessary to notarize, translate, and register these documents. Local bankers or local counsel can provide complete information concerning these details.

Banking, incidentally, is not everywhere the kind of service industry to which we are accustomed in the United States. At home, deposits are the big word, and bank charges are generally quite reasonable for most operations. Overseas, while deposits occasionally generate a small interest credit, surcharges, handling fees, stamp duties, commissions, and premiums amount to sizeable charges. A careful investigation of banking practices and procedures is very much in order before a firm commitment is made to any institution.

Legal Assistance

Consultants are notorious for their occupational independence. They frequently rely on common sense, reasonable judgment, and past experience, and do not readily consult with others outside their profession.

But foreign business liabilities, complicated aspects of tax-related matters, labor laws, and leases, just to mention a few issues, do require expert legal advice. A local attorney should be selected at an early date and acquainted with the consultant's proposed activities in the host country. Even if immediate legal assistance is not needed, it is good to have a lawyer available on short notice. Also, from time to time a consultant requires a local representative to take care of corporate, financial, legal, and other related matters. Competent attorneys can frequently assume these tasks, and will do so against a retainer, a commission, or for a fee. Again, foreign practices differ substantially from those in this country, so you should choose your lawyer as carefully as you pick your banker.

Attention must be paid to other important areas. Has a consultant been engaged to bring the standards of his home experience overseas? Or is he to develop something entirely new that may bring about local improvements in the environment of the host country? He may be required to come forward with solutions to matters of ecology, demography, religious practices, and historic traditions. Frequent consultations with the clients are advisable. Where more than one language is involved, translations should be examined and double checked to make sure they contain no ambiguities. Meetings and conferences, as well as change orders and any departures from agreed upon procedures, need to be recorded and confirmed in writing with notification to all concerned parties.

If the work is performed by the consultant at his home office, it is a good idea to invite representatives of the client to visit and discuss progress at various stages of completion. By the same token, top professionals at home should keep a watchful eye on developments in the field.

The scope of work and terms of reference need to be reviewed time and again. The more check points built into your procedures for monitoring a foreign engagement, the greater your chances of completing the assignment to the full satisfaction of the client, on time, and within the budget.

8

ASSOCIATIONS, JOINT VENTURES, AND REPRESENTATION

International consultants spend great amounts of time discussing the various advantages and disadvantages of forming joint ventures with others, associating with other professionals, establishing foreign partnerships with host-country nationals, and appointing representatives or agents. Circumstances differ from country to country, and there are no simple answers.

Consultants from an industrialized country working in another developed nation will often play a subordinate role. In such cases, pre-contract negotiations will determine the form and extent of organizational collaboration. Only rarely will the choice of association, joint venture, or foreign partnership be made unilaterally by the consultant.

In the developing world, consultants used to hire whatever help they required; pay scales would be in line with local practices and rates. Host-country participation in consulting work was minimal. After World War II, the practice of directly hiring local help at local rates of compensation began to be challenged by foreign employees. The sore point was the discrepancy between the salaries and benefits paid to local employees and the consultant's expatriate staff. In order to avoid discriminatory practices, international consultants began to engage subcontractors, giving preference to host-country nationals and firms. They would then hire their own nationals, paying local salaries but charging the consultant overhead and profit.

Increasingly, during the past 35 years, individuals in the emerging nations demanded full participation in directing and executing projects in their countries. Some were young professionals educated in the industrialized nations; others had accumulated considerable working experience over the years, first as employees of, and then as subcontractors to, international consultants. International consultants found it necessary to associate with qualified local individuals and firms.

Associations and joint ventures can be advantageous to consultants in the following circumstances:

1. There is a genuine need for the combined resources a joint venture provides. The foreign partner contributes experience and technical expertise; the local partner provides reliable analysis of local conditions, customs, and intentions.
2. The project is too ambitious to be undertaken by either firm individually, but will be profitable as a joint venture.
3. The joint venture partners share both professional and philosophical goals.
4. Compatible partners are chosen without undue pressure by clients, governments, financing agencies, or banks.

A partnership, joint venture or representation arrangement that is forced upon a foreign firm does not serve the interests of the host country, the client, or the consultant.

An association may include a partnership, a company, or a corporation that comprises a foreign consultant and host-country individuals or firms. An association may also involve a joint venture of nonresidents and locals who voluntarily, or in order to comply with applicable host-country legislation, set up an entity to perform professional services. This book is not meant to be a guide to the legal requirements of association. In any case, these vary from country to country. An overview of the available options, however, may be useful.

Joining Forces to Find New Business

Associations are sometimes formed simply for the purpose of developing new business. It is extremely difficult even for large consulting firms to cover fully the world's market. When a local associate monitors host-country programs, foreign consultants are well informed about upcoming projects and thus in a good competitive position.

A local partner can also submit his foreign partners' registrations where required, and at times prepare proposal documentation and translations.

When it comes to proposal presentation, negotiations, and contract work, the local associate once again plays an important role. He knows his environment, understands local costs, and can provide accomodations and transportation for his international partners. His knowledge of locally available professional and material support is invaluable.

Some governments demand that a foreign consultant be represented in the country on a permanent basis. This should not discourage you. In my experience, there is no better way to cover an overseas market.

Partners in Overseas Engagements

Deciding to enter, or not to enter, into a local partnership for the execution of a foreign engagement is not easy. There is no choice where host-country legislation makes local participation mandatory. The consultant simply will have to incorporate host-country nationals into his team. The major task then is to locate competent individuals or firms who will fit with you and the project.

When there are no legal requirements for a local partnership, the foreign consultant will have to weigh the advantages and disadvantages of local association. Ask yourself the following questions. Will a local partnership with host-country nationals:

- make it easier, more efficient and more economical to execute the engagement?
- sustain established professional standards?
- mean more or less local interference in the project performance?
- facilitate preferential selection for future projects?

The performance of professional services overseas obliges a consultant to take into account host-country customs. A direct link with local individuals or firms unquestionably leads to a better understanding of the environment.

In most cases, efficiency can be improved through the use of a local partnership. For instance, communications will benefit when a close associate knows the language. Local holidays often not recorded in international calendars will no longer seem to interfere with tight schedules and the visits of foreign executives.

Savings become possible in many areas. Local partners are in a better position to arrange important appointments and meetings. Logistics can be handled according to local custom, and prices will reflect local levels rather than those marked up for the tourist. Where bargaining is a way of life, the expatriate will not be taken advantage of. Administrative details such as bookkeeping, accounting, billings, collections, correspondence, and logistics can be entrusted to host-country nationals, while the expatriates concentrate on their specialized professional tasks.

The international consultant must assess the capabilities of his proposed local associate very carefully. The entire reputation of his firm is at stake, but he can also benefit from local experience.

Clients in the less-developed countries and their lenders frequently accuse architects, engineers, and planners from the industralized nations of overdesigning and underestimating projects. The participation of experienced local people can prevent this. With good management (and close supervision), professionals from different countries can work as one successful team. There are many examples of excellent international partnerships where top professionals work happily with their local counterparts and share responsibility as they would in domestic operations.

Occasionally, consultants are requested to associate locally with individuals and firms who do not seem qualified to do the job. Nothing good comes of these forced marriages, particularly if the foreign consultant is to be held responsible for overall performance. In such a case, it is best to search for an alternative and, if one cannot be agreed upon, to decline the work.

The client's interference in project performance can create difficult situations, particularly when the project is financed by an international bank or agency, and national feelings are inimical to the established terms of reference and scope of work. Should a government change, matters can become complicated too.

It impossible to say if a local association will invite less, or bring more local interference in project performance. Each case will have to be looked at on its own merits. I have found, however, that a competent and professional local partner can be extremely helpful in avoiding or defusing potentially explosive situations. His understanding of events and governmental demands may make it easier to find a solution.

Prospective associates who boast of their political connections are definitely not my choice. They tend to attract more attention than necessary. Whenever somebody tells me that his connections with government, or the party in power, or a particularly outstanding politician assure preferential treatment, I become uneasy. I have seen too many changes of governments, resignations of leaders, and reversals of policy to place my trust in anything but the truly professional qualifications of a partner.

Consultants are generally assigned to perform specific services of limited duration. And as we know, it is not easy to obtain work in the international market place. Repeat engagements from satisfied clients are therefore to be valued above rubies. Competent and respected local partners can be extremely helpful to the international consultant as he builds a foundation for future prospects. Doors will open which remain closed for the majority of outsiders. As foreign consultants are watched and judged through local eyes, a local partner's name on studies, reports, drawings, and specifications will influence judgment. Stationery including both foreign and local firms is proof, particularly in the emerging nations, that the foreign consultant has cooperated closely with the host-country people, and that there is already a common base of mutual confidence. This is of great importance in a world where national fervor is evermore intense.

Another advantage of association overseas is that local partners are usually better able than most outsiders to obtain professional licenses, permits to work, and membership in national societies. These are only three requisites to working abroad that can be time consuming and costly. Local partners may also be able to furnish instruments and equipment, thereby saving costs and eliminating the risk of shipment. At other times, associates are glad to accept, in lieu of payment for services, the instruments and equipment which their foreign partner imported for the execution of the project.

There may be special circumstances that preclude an overseas association. Questions of politics may make it unwise; suitable local partners may not be available; the confidential nature of the project or special contractual limitations may exclude any other outside participation. Otherwise, associating abroad for the execution of an international engagement is highly recommended.

Varieties of Associations and Joint Ventures

Foreign associations, partnerships, or joint ventures may take several forms. Some countries have enacted special legislation limiting the options; others provide only the barest of guidelines. Legal counsel should be sought in the host country in tandem with the consultant's attorneys at home. Whatever the form of the association, the terms need to be worked out in sufficient detail to avoid any later misinterpretations and misunderstandings. Clients may also have to be consulted as to their acceptance of the proposed partnership.

Aside from the mutual obligations, compensation, sharing of profits and losses, tax liabilities, and social obligations, such matters as disputes, arbitration, termination, and assignment clauses require careful attention.

Agreements between consultants may be simple contracts covering specific engagements and limited territory, or broad agreements establishing exclusive rights for extended periods of time. For large undertakings, it is not unusual to establish a new professional entity in the form of a corporation, a limited-liability company, or a partnership.

Where agreements are written to provide specific services for an already existing contract, care should be taken that the clauses of one will not conflict with the stipulations of the other.

When a foreign and a local consultant work together to obtain a project, it is usually not necessary to rush into a formal contract. A simple letter of understanding or consent should specify the general questions that are to be formalized after the job has been received. Sometimes these letters of understanding are required by clients. It is usually quite easy to draft an acceptable document based on common sense and simple language.

Associations and joint ventures are not confined to partnerships of nationals of two countries. There may be groups of four or more different firms—the modus operandi of overseas associations follows no set pattern. Americans, Canadians, and West Germans may team up with Indonesian nationals for a large undertaking in Sumatra. Argentinians, Uruguayans, and Italians are likely to be found working side by side near Asunción with Paraguayan professionals. International joint ventures are often staffed with individuals from many countries. As long as the principal objective of a mixed operation is to provide the best services and to satisfy the client, international consultants will find many possibilities and relatively few limitations in the selection of partners and associates.

Finding the Right Partner

Depending on the country, the search for prospective host-country nationals as associates or partners may be enjoyable or frustrating.

In all industrialized nations, consultants tend to offer their services in the same fashion. Those active internationally participate in conferences and workshops abroad, and are usually well known in consulting circles around the globe. Their professional societies maintain registrations of individuals and firms, and provide information to interested parties. Trade publications carry their professional cards. Yellow pages in the telephone books list them. It is quite easy to locate international consultants in Sweden, the United Kingdom, France, Italy, Germany, and other industrialized nations.

Throughout North and South America, in Europe, the Middle East, and in several Asian countries, competent and experienced professionals are available and can be located. But they are not always established and organized as independent consultants. A foreign professional looking for partners may have to spot individuals and then help them set up a firm or forge a team. Many Latin Americans, particularly, are superbly educated and often internationally experienced; they are mainly interested in getting the chance to practice what they studied while helping in the modernization of their countries. One can find them congregating at universities and colleges. Word of mouth carries fast, especially in the smaller nations, and no major effort is required to meet candidates once it becomes known that international consultants are looking for local participants.

In most of the African nations, and in some Middle Eastern and Asian countries, qualified professionals available to perform private enterprise services are still difficult to find. Individuals with higher degrees are usually employed by governments. Here it can be quite a problem to come upon a suitable partner. Occasionally, university faculty can be persuaded to join a common effort. A carefully worded advertisement in the local press may attract the attention of parents of students who are doing post-graduate work abroad. An enterprising British architect was known for systematically combing Western European and U.S. universities for graduating students of a particular country. He was able to employ several bright young people as junior associates in a project he was executing in their own country.

Government employees in the emerging nations are frequently poorly compensated and often anxious to become independent. It is not unusual to obtain temporary and even permanent releases from government service for host-country professionals, particularly if the consulting engagement is commissioned by the government. From time to time civil servants are able to take a prolonged leave of absence in order to accept an offer from a foreign consultant. Care must be taken in such cases against any misunderstanding with the government agency. Nor should there be a conflict of interest.

It never hurts to talk to as many people as possible when searching for host-country associates. I have more than once established highly satisfactory relations with qualified locals upon the recommendation of the client himself. Several years ago, a minister of state recommended a highly qualified personal friend of his, and I am convinced that the final selection of my firm was influenced by this factor.

Naturally, not all host-country nationals with a professional education will make good partners and associates. Some people cannot perform well as members of a team, others are disinclined to follow directions. Screening of prospective joint venturers is even more important than interviewing employees for international engagements. Academic records must be checked as well as professional registration. Personal references should be requested and investigated. A foreign consultant must not forget that his local associate represents him and his firm.

Beware of the following warning signs that hint at serious difficulties ahead:

1. Pressure to enter a joint venture by governments, clients, or funding sources.
2. Signs in your prospective partner's firm of incompatibility between management and personnel, poor planning, inadequate budgeting of time and finances.
3. Administrative and technical misunderstandings; language difficulties; divergent interpretation of different codes and standards.
4. Higher costs of foreign consultants; differences in the productivity of foreign and local partners.

Representation

Representation is simpler than associations and joint ventures. Here an international consultant appoints a local individual or company to represent himself or his firm. Local legislation often requires that consultants are fully represented locally for prolonged periods of time following professional engagements or even preceding short-listing during a selection process. While professional associations and joint ventures are always acceptable in lieu of representation, qualified individuals may be impossible to find in the less-developed countries. In order to comply with host-country requirements, consultants may be obliged to employ a local non-professional representative. Since he will take on major responsibilities, detailed written agreements should spell out the representative's role, his authority, and his compensation.

A manufacturer's representative in Latin America, for example, may submit letters expressing an interest in upcoming local projects; file documents for official registration; receive invitations to present formal proposals; and provide an authorized, dependable line of communications. A trading company retained as a representative in a country can sponsor visas for foreign visitors and arrange for accommodations, transportation, and translation services as well.

Commercial representatives are much easier to find than qualified professionals. Indeed, there are a great many to choose from almost everywhere. A common sight in some foreign cities is a group of small offices, each displaying a dozen brass name plates of world-renowned multinational corporations. Again, a consultant should carefully examine the credentials of a proposed representative. He should be locally established and of good repute. There must be no conflicts with the representation of competing consultants or suppliers of materials and equipment. He should be able to prove that he can service the consultant's needs.

One more word of caution. Representatives, at times, call themselves agents and propose to enter into agency contracts. In quite a few countries, an agent is regarded (and held accountable) as fully authorized to act for his principals, while a representative acts only within the limits of his specific representation agreement. Legal advice should be sought before entering into any contracts containing a reference to an agent or to agencies. Translations must be particularly clear in this connection.

Compensation

Associates, partners, and joint venturers everywhere around the world must be paid adequately. An early financial agreement between associating consultants is important to establish the business side of a professional relationship.

In all successful international joint ventures, principals and partners must cover their costs and allow for a reasonable profit. It is good policy to set up a contingency fund to cover unexpected reverses. Joint incentive bonuses are also good stimulants for efficiency.

Compensation may be based on actual salaries, benefits, and overhead. Occasionally it may be preferable to establish time rates.

Expenses may be treated as direct or indirect costs according to the nature of each individual engagement. Ideally, all compensation clauses of an association agreement should be compatible with the conditions and terms of the governing client's contract.

If a partnership is entirely equal in terms of man-hours and levels of expertise, an even division of fees is obviously called for. If there are more than two associates involved, or one party furnishes only senior staff compared to many participants at lower working levels provided by others, the matter of adequate compensation requires careful analysis.

I have not experienced major difficulties in reaching amicable agreement with professional consultants regarding payment. Occasionally there have been differences of opinion as to the value attached to the professional responsibility of the lead firm, or the real cost of salaries. Perhaps I have been fortunate. But there has never been an occasion when a frank discussion has not produced a mutually satisfactory conclusion.

Commercial representatives are accustomed to other terms of payment. These may vary from country to country, but generally consist of a monthly retainer plus reimbursement of reasonable expenses, such as postage, telex, cables, messenger costs, registration fees, and stamp duties. Representatives do not normally bill for their overhead, and need not be provided with incentive bonuses.

At times, international consultants are approached by individuals and firms claiming they can obtain engagements for them in return for a retainer, expenses and a commission, or a finder's fee. These offers are sometimes tempting, and every once in a while such a solicitation can produce an engagement. In the vast majority of cases, however, a commercial representative is not in any legitimate position to procure professional services contracts. In any case, a professional consultant's compensation can rarely support commercial commissions or finder's fees. Commercial representatives who provide local support are best paid with a monthly or quarterly lump-sum retainer plus expenses.

Accounting and Bookkeeping

Almost every sovereign country has legislation requiring income-producing enterprises to maintain books according to authorized accounting procedures. Whenever an international consultant establishes a legal entity to perform services in a host country, at least some minimum accounting demands will have to be met.

Clients and their financiers frequently demand the right to inspect their consultants' books. A few international development agencies stipulate that detailed records be kept available several years after the completion of an engagement. In these circumstances, there is no choice. But if associations, joint ventures, and partnerships with host-country individuals or third-country nationals are not locally incorporated or registered, accounting and bookkeeping systems of the parties are matters of internal agreement among the parties.

Wherever a foreign consultant is subject to host-country taxation, it will be in his best interest to maintain complete records and carefully file covering vouchers. When the international consultant is subject to one kind of taxation and his host-country partner to another—something that occurs quite frequently—special books and separate accounts must be kept. When a joint venture sends its clients unified bills, the partners must arrange for the internal distribution of funds.

Accounting procedures in foreign lands can be time consuming and costly. Many international consultants forego legal incorporation and formal partnership status wherever possible to escape the administrative demands of bookkeeping abroad. This does not mean that joint venturers should not keep records for the purpose of accounting and controls. But these can be held to whatever is required for internal monitoring.

Dos and Don'ts

The advantages and disadvantages of joining forces with others abroad or going it alone must be considered for every project in a new country, and for many repeat engagements as well. Here are a few key DO'S and DON'TS for successful overseas partnerships:

DO —   Carefully investigate your proposed future associates. Make sure of their standing in their community, their professional integrity, and financial stability.
Provide fast and efficient channels of communication. Designate fully capable people for liaison on your side and request the same from your associates.
Be certain there is full understanding on policies, authority, and responsibility. Set up procedures early; avoid leaving important decisions for later.
Strive for the highest level of performance. Demand it from your associates as you expect it from members of your own firm.

Slow down to think out and discuss your problems. Give your associates an opportunity to catch up and understand.

DON'T —   Select anyone as an associate overseas with whom you would not associate with at home. Compromising on standards and ethics invites serious trouble.

Make promises that cannot be met.

Assume you have all the answers. Listen carefully to your associates' opinions. You may benefit from their local experience.

Maintain two different sets of figures and books. Have a definite and realistic concept of costs, expenses, and profits, and be sure your associates understand and concur.

Impose domestic procedures on your overseas associates if they are not vital to the success of the project.

9

TERMINATING CONTRACTS, DISPUTES, FORCE MAJEURE, AND INTERNATIONAL ARBITRATION

As far as the actual work goes, overseas consulting is not in itself different than doing professional work domestically. But extraordinary and unforeseen events far from home may test the management skills and stamina of the international consultant and his foreign client. Natural disasters, economic crises, and political upheavals must be anticipated in many parts of the world. Since even the best-laid plans are frequently subject to change, international contracts should provide equitable procedures for adapting to new circumstances.

Let us examine a number of the special conditions that ought to be included in international consulting agreements.

Terminating Contracts

A termination clause in a professional services contract reserves to the client the right to terminate the consultant's work upon due notice for convenience, default, or force majeure. It defines the obligations of the consultant upon receipt of such notice, as well as the consultant's right to compensation in the event of each type of termination. For example, in the case of termination for convenience, the clause should provide for compensation to the consultant for all expenses incurred in good faith for his performance of the contract up to the point of termination, and for a reasonable fee, plus all termination expenses. In case of default by the consultant, the client should not be held responsible for payments beyond the consultant's accepted and approved performance. Should the client default in payment to the consultant, the client must assume all termination costs and indemnify the consultant to the extent of their specific agreement. Finally, in the case of force majeure, termination of contracts usually is governed by an agreement that the client accepts billings from the consultants for all reasonable expenses up to the time of notification, plus termination costs but excluding unearned fees.

I should emphasize that a client can terminate a consultant with or without cause, but that a consultant can normally terminate only for non-payment, or force-majeure, unless additional clauses in the contract specifically spell out other defaults by the client which could lead to termination by the consultant.

Disputes

Disputes are most likely to involve matters of professional judgment. International work is complicated by intangible factors of human temperament, involuntary misunderstanding, different educational backgrounds, poor communications, erroneous interpretation of data, and language problems. Dispute clauses establish the procedure to be followed when a dispute arises under the terms of a contract.

A quick settlement of differences of judgment should be stipulated as a first step. Project managers can sometimes propose settlements of disputes which, if left unattended, would grow into major fights. Another relatively easy procedure that avoids major costs is the appointment of a neutral mediator. (The mediator may have the authority to enforce a ruling.)

Since attempts at conciliation do not always succeed, it is a good idea to prescribe a second procedure for reconciling the difference in that case. The contract should stipulate official mediation (either binding or non-binding). Finally, the contract must specify the steps to be followed if the case has to be arbitrated. Arbitration is binding and conducted in a formal manner in compliance with rules and regulations of the International Court of Arbitration or arbitration societies and associations.

Dispute clauses should also establish the method of appealing any decision when the procedure involved does not call for a binding decision.

Force Majeure

The *American Heritage Dictionary of the English Language* defines force majeure as "an unexpected or uncontrolled event that upsets one's plans or releases one from obligations." Contract language needs to be more specific. Agreement will have to be reached with a client as to what constitutes force majeure in his particular country.

An eight-inch rainfall within twenty-four hours in Western Europe may well be regarded as a major disaster qualifying as force majeure. In the rain forests of northeastern Brazil or in Liberia, this is a daily possibility during the rainy season. Strikes and lockouts are common occurrences in many industrial countries. Civil disturbances, riots, and political upheaval, all of which can seriously interupt consulting work, are more likely to occur in the developing nations.

Force majeure clauses are necessary to define acts beyond the control of the client and the consultant. They establish the conditions which would excuse a consultant, temporarily or permanently, from performing all or part of his obligations; they similarly apply to the client under the same conditions. Force majeure clauses also prescribe the procedures that should be followed by both client and consultant in determining and giving due notification in case force majeure is invoked. They set forth the consultant's and the client's rights and obligations with regard to temporary suspension of work, payment of compensation and expenses, evacuation of personnel, and transport of instruments and equipment. Finally, force majeure clauses should state the appropriate steps to be taken in case of consequent contract termination.

International Arbitration

The administration of justice is slow and expensive everywhere in the world. In nations where judges are appointed politically, it can be extremely difficult to pursue legitimate grievances. Time-consuming reviews and obligatory appeals follow original judgments under some countries' legal codes. In my judgment there is no question that arbitration is a better alternative for consultants than going to court.

Because of worldwide concern about international arbitration, the 1975 Conference on Security and Cooperation in Europe, generally referred to as "Helsinki," adopted a resolution strongly recommending private commercial arbitration to resolve international trade disputes. The resolution urged the inclusion of arbitration clauses in commercial contracts, industrial cooperation contracts, and in special agreements; recommended that international contracts provide for arbitration under a mutually acceptable set of rules; and strongly suggested that arbitration be permitted in a third country. (Arbitration is still rejected by a number of sovereign governments despite the Helsinki Resolution's recommendations and United Nations support of the process.)

An international consultant should, wherever possible, include a provision in his service contract for the arbitration of disputes and claims by an impartial body. Remember that some nations do not recognize arbitration, and others may prohibit intervention by internationally recognized authorities. If alternative arrangements are not feasible, you should seek legal counsel about how you can protect yourself against costly and dilatory court proceedings.

International bodies offering arbitration services should be cited in consulting agreements when arbitration is agreed upon. These include:

The Court of Arbitration
International Chamber of Commerce
38 Courts Albert ler
Paris, France 75008

The American Arbitration Association
140 West 51st Street
New York, NY 10020

World Arbitration Institute
140 West 51st Street
New York, NY 10020

Both the Court of Arbitration of the International Chamber of Commerce and the American Arbitration Association provide the services of qualified individual arbitrators. They have also promulgated rules and regulations that will make for orderly arbitration proceedings, fair hearings, and proper decisions. UNCITRAL has also recently formulated arbitration rules and model clauses. International financial institutions and development agencies have also developed language that I highly recommend as a guideline for agreements in both the public and private sector.

Another institution offering arbitration services is the International Centre for Settlement of Investment Disputes (ICSID). Established in 1965 by the Convention on the Settlement of Investment Disputes between States and Nationals of Other States, the Centre functions as an autonomous member of the World Bank group in Washington. The Centre serves parties for settling international investment disputes.

As a number of sovereign nations do not accept arbitration clauses in official contracts and will not honor arbitration awards outside their court systems, the conciliation and arbitration facilities offered by ICSID are highly regarded by the international consulting sector. (A high percentage of all consulting work overseas is connected to investment activities.)

The following states, as of 1986, officially recognize, and are disposed towards acceptance of, ICSID conciliation and arbitration services:

Afghanistan	Guinea
Australia	Guyana
Austria	Haiti
Bangladesh	Iceland
Barbados	Indonesia
Belgium	Ireland
Benin, Peoples' Republic of	Israel
Botswana	Italy
Burkina-Faso	Ivory Coast
Burundi	Jamaica
Cameroon	Japan
Central African Republic	Jordan
Chad	Kenya
Comoros	Korea, Republic of
Congo, Peoples' Republic of the	Kuwait
Costa Rica	Lesotho
Cyprus	Liberia
Denmark	Luxembourg
Egypt	Madagascar
El Salvador	Malawi
Ethiopia	Malaysia
Fiji	Mali
Finland	Mauritania
France	Mauritius
Gabon	Morocco
Gambia	Nepal
Germany, Federal Republic	Netherlands
Ghana	New Zealand
Greece	Niger

Nigeria
Norway
Pakistan
Papua New Guinea
Paraguay
Philippines
Portugal
Romania
Rwanda
Saudi Arabia
Senegal
Seychelles
Sierra Leone
Singapore
Solomon Islands
Somalia
Sri Lanka

St. Lucia
Sudan
Swaziland
Sweden
Switzerland
Togo
Trinidad and Tobago
Tunisia
Uganda
United Arab Emirates
United Kingdom
United States
Western Samoa
Yugoslavia
Zaire
Zambia

Where some nations in Latin America and the Middle East do not permit arbitration clauses in their contracts, consultants are well advised to consult host-country attorneys and develop a means to resolve potential disputes through out-of-court proceedings.

The language of arbitration clauses varies from country to country and from case to case.

It is a truism that contracts are only as good as the good will of the contracting parties. Still, honest differences of opinion and judgment do occur. Making sure that contracts include clauses for speedy and satisfactory settlements of disagreements is an essential matter of self-protection for the international consultant.

10

PROFESSIONAL LIABILITY, INSURANCE, BONDS, AND GUARANTEES

Professional Liability

Professionals in the United States are caught up in a legal explosion. The practice of consulting is vulnerable in ways it has not been before to liability charges and suits.

The charge of professional negligence is a very serious matter. Even if the claims finally prove to be without merit and the consultant is fully vindicated, the proceedings themselves are burdensome, and damage to one's professional reputation can be lasting and irreparable. The cost of defending a liability suit can easily exceed the total fee earned during the engagement.

Litigation, of course, begins with a controversy. Professional liability claims do not only result from disputes in professional areas of expertise; they are frequently caused by a failure of communications and deteriorating relations between the consultant and his client. Minor clashes tend to be cumulative and, if left unresolved, can lead to litigation, termination, and penalties.

Legal proceedings overseas against international professionals, while still relatively rare, are increasing. A serious dispute between a foreign consultant and his overseas client can put the consultant on a blacklist for any further engagements in the country. Most of the international financing institutions and development agencies maintain performance records on all consultants working on projects that receive institutional support. Charges of professional negligence, omissions and errors, or poor judgment leveled against a consulting firm in a Latin American country may therefore have repercussions in South Asia.

Liability suits in the United States are increasingly resolved by panels of arbitration or in courts of law. Out-of-court settlements are fairly rare in the United States. But in foreign disputes involving consulting practices and professional judgment, international consultants are often obliged to institute remedial action. This demands time-consuming trips, costly reviews, and possibly additional work for which reasonable compensation cannot be collected.

The extraordinary number of suits brought against consulting engineers in the United States has led to sharply higher premium costs. In some cases, companies refuse to insure at all. This has prompted a new industry-wide initiative—unified risk insurance. Contractors' liability, product liability, and completed-operations insurance are included in one policy covering all members of the design and construction team. The whole entity—owners, architects, engineers, contractors, and subs—is considered responsible as a unit when damages are awarded. Third-party claims are defended by a single insurer. Because one insurer covers the entire team, the expense of defending individuals on a claim-by-claim basis is eliminated, making insurance coverage more efficient.

The most important step you can take to avoid liability problems is to make sure that communications on all levels are well established, perfectly understood, and painstakingly maintained from the moment you first meet the client until final receipt of a letter of acceptance marking the official conclusion of the assignment. Tact, diplomacy, and an understanding of human relations are all important. Technical lapses can be avoided through vigilant monitoring; difficulties caused by misunderstandings, human factors, and cultural differences should be handled delicately before they prejudice future relationships and threaten harmonious cooperation.

Professional liability insurance policies are available to most established consultants, although premiums are substantial. Naturally, they increase as claims accumulate. Deductibles vary but also tend to be high. Insurance companies throughout the world have not as yet differentiated between domestic and foreign risks when the consultant is considered insurable. Strictly domestic policies, however, should be endorsed to cover international engagements. Riders can be written for specific work abroad, and world-wide coverage is available to established individuals and firms from insurers in many countries. Agencies of the governments of Germany, France, Great Britain, and Japan, among others, underwrite special risks for their nationals, particularly when services are provided to an officially recognized host-government entity.

Associations, joint ventures, and partnerships with foreign individuals and firms are not normally included in standard professional liability insurance policies. You must apply for and obtain adequate protection to cover the risks and responsibilities of each of the multinational partners in a joint venture.

Insurance coverage for professional liability overseas is frequently written into a domestic policy in the form of an endorsement. Separate policies are sometimes issued for large overseas engagements. In either case, consultants should instruct their insurance agents to include coverage for hazards endemic to an international practice: the high costs of communications and travel, expenses of mobilization and demobilization, legal fees charged by domestic and foreign attorneys, translations, and the issuance of bonds and guarantees.

In extreme instances of liability claims, a client may confiscate his foreign consultant's physical assets and freeze his funds. As the final disposition of a complicated overseas case may take a long time, a consultant would benefit from insurance coverage for this contingency.

The newcomer with little professional liability insurance experience may find it useful to have the names and addresses of some companies who sell policies to consultants in the United States:

Continental Casualty Co. (CNA), Victor O. Schinnerer & Co., Inc., 5028 Wisconsin Ave., N.W., Washington, DC 20016; (202) 885-9500.

INAPRO (CIGNA), P.O. Box 2353, 127 John St., New York, NY 10272; (212) 556-5000.

Design Professionals Insurance Corp. (DPIC), P.O. Drawer DPFC, Monterey, CA 93942; (408) 649-5522.

Imperial Casualty & Indemnity Co., Professional Coverage Managers, Inc., 130 Williams St., New York, NY 10038; (212) 619-4900.

Lloyds of London, R.B. Jones, 175 West Jackson Blvd., Chicago, IL 60604; (312) 435-6200.

Comstock Insurance, Professional Managers, Inc., 2 North Riverside Plaza, Chicago, IL 60606; (312) 559-0101.

General Accident, Shand Morahan, 1 American Plaza, Evanston, IL 60201; (312) 866-2800.

Insurance

Insurance companies in the United States are not always able or willing to write policies that fully satisfy a consultant's needs, but Lloyd's of London and other international insurance brokers serve the needs of many individuals and firms throughout the world. As long as professional liability constitutes an element of risk, consultants should protect themselves with the most comprehensive insurance coverage that can be obtained at a reasonable premium.

Other chapters refer to insurance. The following is a guideline to areas of foreign risk for which international consultants should consider full or partial overseas coverage.

Comprehensive General Liability
Umbrellas
Legal Liability
Professional Benefit Liability

Commercial Credit Risks: Client's failure to pay
          Client's insolvency

Political Risks: Failure to transfer local funds
      into foreign exchange
      Cancellation of licenses or permits
      War, hostilities, civil war, rebellion, revolution,
       insurrection, civil commotion
      Requisition, expropriation, confiscation,
       intervention
Joint Ventures, Associations
Medical, Hospitalization, Life
Accident, Personal Injury
Travel Accident
Property, Housing, Offices,
 and Personal Belongings: Fire, lightning, explosion, vandalism
           Earthquake, flood
           Political risk

Investments: Commercial risk
      Political risk
Kidnapping, Extortion
Inflation Risk

Comprehensive general liability covers all liability arising out of declared occupation hazards, and specifically includes the cost of defense. For overseas work, I recommend adding false arrest, libel, slander, and defamation of character.

Umbrella policies are useful when high policy limits are needed, but unless premiums rise sharply, this coverage may not be easily obtainable in the future.

Legal liability should be validated for the employment of foreign counsel in addition to the normal domestic legal assistance.

Employee liability is partially covered through United States workmen's compensation, but should be extended for international work either through the consultant's carrier or host-country institutions. Employee-benefit liability for foreign engagements covers the consultant's overseas expatriate staff and may also cover employees of third countries, host-country employees, and expatriates under the laws of the host country. Insurance is definitely warranted when host-country legislation provides more benefits than the consultant's own government or social security agency.

Commercial credit risks, as well as political risks, are insurable in the United States by the Foreign Credit Insurance Association (FCIA) and the Export-Import Bank. A number of industralized nations have similar government-sponsored insurance available through official export credit agencies. These include COFACE in France, Hermes Kreditversicherung GmBH in Germany, and ECGD in Great Britain. Commercial and political risk coverage generally requires official backing from host-government agencies. Many, but not all, of the less-developed nations have expressed their readiness to issue government guarantees in return for the availability of this kind of insurance. Consultants should check with their insurance brokers to make sure that commercial and political risks in a particular country are insurable.

All policies should always be current, renewals negotiated in good time, and additions assured before new contracts are signed. The following points are a general checklist for keeping your coverage up to date.

1. Request a report from your insurance agent or company outlining premium increases and coverage reductions anticipated on renewal.
2. Be sure future bids reflect expected premium increases and coverage reductions.
3. Begin negotiating your renewal at least three or four months prior to expiration. Prepare a clear and persuasive submission.
4. Consider requesting proposals from other companies based on similar insurance specifications.

5. Focus on desirable coverages you wish to renew, especially in liability areas.
6. Review umbrella limits and adjust them if necessary.
7. Apply a risk factor when comparing worker's compensation dividend programs to such alternatives as retrospective rating plans, self-insurance, and captives.
8. Review alternate funding programs such as association plans, self-insurance, and captives.
9. Review contract documents for possible risk-management improvement.
10. Review and rethink, if necessary, your approach to risk management and safety.

Medical, hospitalization, life, accident, and personal injury insurance should be similar to domestic practice. Make sure that overseas charges will be accepted by the insurance carriers for illness and accidents occuring overseas. Medical evacuation costs for employees and their dependents may also have to be included.

Travel accident coverage should specifically permit foreign travel and provide for higher limits than equivalent domestic insurance policies.

Property, housing, offices, and personal belongings of the consultant and his employees warrant extended coverage that includes some risks not commonly named in domestic insurance documents. Flood insurance was extremely hard to obtain in the United States before the government stepped in and established a special program. In some countries, however, flood insurance is nothing out of the ordinary and commands a negligible premium.

Investment insurance is similar to political and commercial risk insurance and is handled, if not totally by government agencies, at least in part with official support. U.S. consultants seeking coverage for investments overseas should familiarize themselves with programs sponsored by the Overseas Private Investment Corporation (OPIC) in Washington.

Terrorism, unfortunately, has become a constant threat in the past decade. Prominent consultants have been targets of subversive groups in several countries. Large sums of money are sought in return for the release of kidnap victims. Ransom demands well exceed the life savings of most professionals, and few consulting firms are in the position to meet them.

Kidnap insurance has existed for many years in the private sector, but the recent wave of extortion and kidnappings has forced consultants to develop an acute interest in this kind of coverage. Obviously, a kidnapping policy is a two-edged sword. Should its existence become known, disaster might be invited rather than averted. Consultants will have to choose on the basis of their particular circumstances. Unhappily, the risk of terrorism cannot be entirely ignored.

Inflation risk insurance is furnished almost exclusively by a few governments through quasi-official agencies. The idea was pioneered by France many years ago and took on increasing importance in those markets where price is an important factor in securing an engagement. COFACE's efforts were matched for a time by the Japanese and other ambitious government exporters of services. The U.S. government has flatly refused to support inflation risk insurance, arguing that it is illegal in international trade. Consultants entering into contracts extending over several years in inflation-prone nations should at least investigate the availability of this somewhat unusual coverage.

The field of insurance in general is complicated and highly specialized. Insurance brokers are often respected businessmen themselves and should be fully consulted in matters relating to risks prevailing in international activities.

Insurance premiums are charged to overhead accounts and qualify more often than not as directly reimbursable project costs.

Bonds and Guarantees

Design contractors and general contractors have traditionally furnished bonds to guarantee bids, project performance, payment advances, materials, general workmanship, and equipment used in the development of physical facilities.

Consultants whose work consists of intellectual services are not customarily required to place bonds or provide guarantees. Professionals do not bid for contracts; they propose to provide services and then negotiate detailed agreements. While professional consultants specify materials and equipment, they do not assume responsibility for their manufacture and installation.

Occasionally consultants are required by clients to provide a bank guarantee or a bond in return for the receipt of advance payments or the establishment of revolving funds. This is not an unreasonable demand and should be met without major difficulties. Banks abroad underwrite guarantees for a small consideration, and insurance companies in many parts of the world issue surety bonds at reasonable premiums.

During the past decade, international consultants performing professional services abroad have come under pressure by powerful clients in the third world to bid for contracts and to secure them with bank guarantees or surety bonds.

Controversy over the quality of intellectual performance is extremely difficult to resolve because it involves qualitative professional judgment. Few observers in the emerging nations have the experience, qualification, and independence to determine if a foreign consultant has indeed failed in the execution of his contractual duties to the extent that his performance bond should be called.

Furthermore, demands for bank performance-guarantees draw directly on a professional's line of credit, limit his working capital, and greatly increase the financial risks of such an undertaking. There have been credible reports of guarantees of five to ten percent on bid bonds; five to fifteen percent of the total project cost for performance; and, at times, an additional ten percent for retention certificates payable from six months to several years after the completion of the work.

Despite the inherent pitfalls of bidding for contracts and providing bonds, the lure of lucrative work has tempted some international consultants to accept professional engagements on non-professional terms. To make the process more palatable to consultants, clients and their financiers have developed the two envelope system where a shortlisted consultant seals his professional proposal in one envelope and his price in another. The client opens the price envelope in the consultant's presence, after he has been notified that it is the first choice. A number of governments from the industrialized nations, notably the Japanese, encourage their nationals to bid on bonded contracts by underwriting guarantees on a government-to-government basis.

As a rule, bonds and guarantees are readily available to international consultants. Although the U.S. banking system is prevented from extending credit guarantees under the current law, surety bonds are commonly furnished within the United States and for international engagements. Banks in Europe, Hong Kong, Singapore, Japan, Panama, and the Bahamas, as well as other countries, sell guarantees as a commercial service. When letters of credit are accepted in lieu of bonds and guarantees, they can be obtained through any major U.S. bank. In some countries, including the United States, insurance is now available to cover a consultant's letter of credit against unjustified drawings.

Although I have been reluctant to bid for contracts or to provide performance bonds and guarantees other than to cover payment advances and revolving funds, these are matters that professional consultants must judge for themselves.

11

INTERNATIONAL DEVELOPMENT INSTITUTIONS AND FINANCING AGENCIES

Many international consulting services are financed by the international development institutions and financing agencies. While the governments of some industralized nations have established export credit agencies to stimulate export of goods and services, the major international organizations are the chief providers of assistance to the less-developed countries.

The heavy burden of foreign debt accrued by many nations has made private, investment-banking, and industrial sources reluctant to assume financial risks without some kind of protection. This, combined with the ever-increasing pressure in less-developed countries to step up the pace of development in the face of population increases and demands for better services and facilities, has inspired new concepts of financing. Co-financing, parallel financing, and the extension of guarantees and special credits allows complex combinations of capital resources. International development financing today is a mix of private enterprise, merchant banking, investment companies, and development institutions.

Consultants providing professional services overseas must recognize the importance of the international financing institutions. While governments to a large extent develop the concept of a project, provide the work, and select the consultants, the financial institutions supply the funds. As bankers, they dictate many of the terms and conditions under which the projects are to be approached and developed. They will review contracts, consultants, contractors, and suppliers and question choices as well as conditions and fees.

Relationships between the lenders and the borrowers are normally quite good. Few borrowers have been known to successfully defy the lender's rules and regulations. Still, differences of interpretation and changing circumstances often cause serious reappraisal. Consultants should take the lead when it comes to project discussions between borrowers and lenders, and must therefore fully understand the role of both parties. A grasp of the inner workings of the lending agency is of great importance for the successful execution of an internationally-financed engagement.

Who actually engages an international consultant? Is it the client, the borrower (who may be the client's government), or the lender (who may be an international development institution)? What is the exact role of the various institutions and agencies? How do they function? To whom is the independent consultant responsible? Who is really in charge? What happens when financiers instruct the consultant to follow practices and procedures that neither he nor his client would choose? What happens to the traditional relationship of consultant and client when the financier has separate relationships with both client and consultant?

This chapter deals in considerable detail with the international development institutions and financing agencies as they affect the overseas consulting community. Much of the following information has been furnished by these organizations, who are as anxious as the consultants to foster understanding and establish good will, which serves the best interest of everyone involved in international development.

United Nations Development Programme (UNDP)

1 United Nations Plaza
New York, NY 10017
U.S.A.
Tel.: (212) 754-1234
Telex: 236 286 (DPNY-UR)
Cables: UNDEVPRO New York

Many international agencies who commission consulting services are linked to the United Nations through the United Nations Development Programme, which is therefore a major force in international development.

UNDP works with 150 governments and 35 international agencies to promote higher standards of living and economic growth throughout the developing areas of the world. Its origins go back to the 1950s. In 1966 the UN General Assembly created UNDP to plan, administer, and finance technical cooperation and feasibility studies (pre-investment and investment support projects). UNDP currently provides financial and technical support to more than 5,000 projects in agriculture, industry, education, power production, transport, communications, public administration, health, housing, trade, and other related fields. Approximately 55% of UNDP assistance goes to countries where the per capita gross national product is under $200.

Project work covers five main categories:

1. Surveying and assessing natural resources; industrial, commercial and export potentials; and other development assets.

2. Stimulating capital investment to develop resources.

3. Training in vocational and professional skills.

4. Transferring appropriate technologies and stimulating the growth of local technological capabilities.

5. Economic and social planning.

Most projects are designed to be self-continuing, with national personnel taking over as UNDP support is phased out. About 60% of project cost is furnished by the recipient countries through provision of national personnel, project buildings and facilities, and locally available supplies and services. The remaining 40% is financed by UNDP, whose budget comes from voluntary contributions by virtually every member of the UN or its affiliated agencies.

UNDP maintains country offices in more than 100 developing nations. These are headed by resident representatives who have a great deal of responsibility for program operations.

UNDP assistance is integrated into national or regional development efforts, and almost all of its projects are carried out by the United Nations itself or one of its participant agencies. The UNDP executes a limited number of projects directly, as do certain recipient governments. Procurement services are handled directly at UNDP Headquarters, and, for field offices, are normally executed through the United Nations Purchases and Transportation Service.

The UNDP Office for Projects Execution (OPE) oversees those projects which do not fall directly within the field of competence of any particular agency. These include interdisciplinary and multipurpose projects; projects in specialized or advanced technology; those involving two or more agencies in regional or physical-planning projects requiring general management or special direction; and selected projects which governments might want UNDP to implement directly.

UNDP-assisted projects are relatively small, usually averaging from $1 million to $1.5 million. But they often generate heavy capital investment of tens to hundreds of millions of dollars. So far, UNDP-assisted pre-investment studies have generated over $43 billion in follow-up investment. These outlays are being used for major construction projects, such as transport systems, dams, telecommunication networks, major agricultural schemes, new industries, and many other developments.

How UNDP Projects Originate

Technical assistance grants over a five-year period are first estimated for a developing country. This estimate is known as the Indicative Planning Figure (IPF). The recipient government then draws up a country program based on development objectives. Projects in specific fields such as agriculture, education, or health are proposed at this stage.

The executing agency of the United Nations that will implement the project is jointly determined by the recipient country and the funding organization. In some exceptional cases, execution and implementation may be carried out by the funding organization (UNDP) directly. When a project is approved, the executing agency begins procurement.

Advance Notice of UNDP-Financed Business Opportunities

Dissemination of advance information on business opportunities is a prime concern of the United Nations Development Programme. Early notice means increased competition for contract awards and lower costs. Equitable geographical distribution of procurement sources is also possible.

A primary source of information on UNDP-financed business opportunities is the *Development Forum/Business Edition (DFBE*, published twenty-four times a year by the United Nations Division for Economic and Social Information/Department of Public

Information [DESI/DPI]). This periodical provides information on international business opportunities based upon data furnished by the UNDP, the executing and specialized agencies, the World Bank, the regional development banks, and some bilateral development programs.

Notices generally give details of contracts for services, goods, equipment, and construction required for the particular projects described, as well as instructions for obtaining tender documents or gaining consideration as a potential supplier. Contacts for each advertised project are listed so consultants can make direct inquiries.

The *Development Forum/Business Edition* is available to the public through annual subscription. Inquiries regarding subscriptions should be directed to:

DESI/DPI	or	Development Forum
United Nations		Liaison Unit, Room E-1035
Palais des Nations		World Bank
CH01211 Geneva 10		Washington, D.C. 20433
Switzerland		U.S.A.

Projects cannot always be fully publicized. Firms should contact the various executing agencies of the UN development system, governments, and resident representatives of UNDP for advance information they may have about forthcoming projects.

Selection Process

Information concerning the selection process should be obtained from the appropriate executing agency. The selection process followed by UNDP/OPE, which is described here, may vary from agency to agency.

A qualified consultant is often hired for a short-term mission to the project country accompanied by the project management officer as necessary to evaluate the technical requirements. Detailed terms of reference specifying all technical and administrative requirements are then prepared in consultation with the government. Pertinent documentation is then sent to the firms invited to submit separate technical and price proposals. For large projects, twenty or thirty firms may be screened to reach the usual short list of three or six firms asked to enter the normal competitive proposal process. To ensure that all qualified firms are given the opportunity to be short listed, considerations other than technical competence are also reviewed. These include equitable geographical distribution, past performance records, and national preferences of the host country.

OPE has a data base of some 2,500 firms stored in its own computer, refers to other rosters as necessary, and is also associated with the World Bank registration system. Four to eight weeks are normally allowed for submission of proposals. The proposals are evaluated by officials on a weighted point system covering such items as firm reputation, international and regional experience, approach and work plan, methodology, personnel, and project management.

Contract Awards

Following evaluation and rating of firms, a written and oral presentation is made to the UNDP Contracts Committee requesting its advice on OPE's recommendation to enter negotiations with the selected firm. The process of evaluation is intended to assist in upgrading the quality of the selected firm's proposal during contract negotiations.

The firms or organizations on the short list must normally be cleared by the recipient government. Should a government request the deletion of a firm, another one is substituted.

After satisfactory negotiations, a contract is signed between OPE and the selected firm. The entire process, from receipt of project document to the arrival of the team in the field, usually takes three or four months. In cases of particular urgency, the process may be reduced to three months or less. In some emergency cases, which require special approval, projects have been implemented in weeks.

United Nations Development Programme Office for Projects Execution (OPE)

Senior Director, Office for Projects Execution
United Nations Development Programme
Room FF 0994
1 United Nation Plaza
New York, NY 10017
U.S.A.
Tel. (212) 754-3125
Telex: 429074 undpope and
          645495 undpope nyk

Procedure

Virtually all technical assistance projects are implemented through subcontracts with consulting firms. Eventually, OPE will use the computerized consultant rosters of the World Bank, but in the interim it maintains its own roster of consultants. The normal pattern of selection procedure is as follows:

1. OPE requests informal expressions of interest from a selected short list of three to five firms, which the recipient government approves. Those who respond are placed on the official short list with additional firms solicited until the short list is complete. Each firm is then given terms of reference, the available budget, and the names of all the competitors;
2. Firms are required to submit technical proposals and prices in separate envelopes;
3. The technical proposals are ranked by OPE on the following points basis:
   50 percent for the team (with 15 percent for the team leader),
   10 percent for the firm,
   40 percent for the method of approaching the task.
4. The prices of the firm with the most acceptable technical offer are considered.

A decision is normally made within ten days of submission of offers. Upon request, OPE will tell unsuccessful firms why their offers were rejected.

Food and Agriculture Organization of the United Nations (FAO)

Chief, Contracts Branch
Administrative Services Division
Food and Agriculture Organization of the United Nations
Via Delle Terme di Caracalla
00100 Rome, Italy
Tel.: 57591
Telex: 610181 FAOI
Cable: FOODAGRI Rome

Fields of activity include studies for the development of soil and water resources for agricultural development; promotion of the global exchange of improved and new plant species and their introduction; the spreading of advanced agricultural techniques; the expansion and improvement of animal husbandry and the combatting of animal diseases; the development and utilization of the resources of the sea; applied research into nutrition and food science; soil erosion control; the expansion of training and extension services; processing, storage and marketing of agricultural, forestry and fishing products; the improvement of hide, skin and leather production; land reclamation and resettlement; pilot schemes and demonstration projects in the field of rural development; development of forest industries; irrigation engineering; control of agricultural pests and diseases and use of fertilizers; socioeconomic studies related to rural development.

Project Implementation

Contract services required by the Organization are almost exclusively in connection with field projects funded by the United Nations Development Programme, Funds-in-Trust Programme, Technical Cooperation Programme, and Food Security Assistance Scheme. Contracts are undertaken for those services which are not available within the Organization, but the Organization may also decide to subcontract all or part of a project with respect to services which are available within the Organization.

Contract Award Procedures

Contracts are usually awarded on the basis of international competition. If the contract is for such matters as charter of aircraft, aerial photography, topography, and drilling, for which the organization can establish precise and detailed specifications, sealed bids are requested. The number of firms asked to bid is determined in consultation with the technical office requesting services and may be subject to the agreement of the recipient government.

For economic and feasibility studies, civil engineering, and forestry inventories, where precise specifications cannot be established by the Organization, uncosted technical proposals are requested, and the budgetary allocation of such contract is provided to the competing firms. The number of proposals invited is restricted to a short list of three approved by an interdepartmental committee of the Organization, subject to the approval of the recipient government.

In turn-key installations requiring engineering services in addition to the supply of equipment, the Organization requests costed technical proposals from a short list of six or seven firms which compete on the basis of performance and budget specifications. In all cases primary consideration is given to those firms and organizations which are registered with the Organization and have submitted a written expression of interest in the proposed contract. This must include the number and title of the project, the country in which it will be implemented, and the funding agency.

When requesting technical proposals, the Organization may decide to use the two-envelope system in which a technical evaluation and a financial evaluation are made independently. The technical evaluation is made by the division concerned. Only after the contracts branch has received the technical evaluation are the second envelopes, containing the financial proposals, opened.

Preference may be given to consulting firms forming joint ventures with local firms. In such cases, this will be specifically stated in the letter of invitation to bid.

Sources of Information and Expressions of Interest

In the past, because contract services required by the Organization were funded almost exclusively by United Nations Development Programme projects, announcement of future contracts could be found in *Development Forum/Business Edition*.

With increased funding for field projects coming from other sources, the organization is considering how to give interested parties information on contracts funded by all sources.

International Fund for Agricultural Development (IFAD)

107 Via del Serafico
00142 Rome
Italy
Tel.: (06) 54591
Telex: 614160/2
Cable: IFAD Rome

IFAD is a specialized agency of the United Nations created in 1977 as a special source of development finance for the agricultural sector. It helps developing countries expand their food production,

improve nutrition, and combat rural poverty. It works closely with
FAO, the World Bank, and the regional development banks. Appraisal of IFAD projects and administration of its loans are normally entrusted to one of these institutions. Projects financed so far
include integrated rural development; food production; irrigation
(with particular emphasis on on-farm development); fisheries; agricultural credit; pasture and livestock development; and agricultural
support services, including research.

Procedure

IFAD does not maintain its own register of consulting firms, but
relies on those of other institutions. Consultants are selected under
procedures similar to those of the other institutions. Consultants
engaged by borrowers are selected in accordance with the procedures of the international financial institution administering IFAD's
loan.

World Health Organization (WHO)

Environmental Technology & Support
Division of Environmental Health
World Health Organization
Avenue Appia
1211 Geneva 27 Switzerland
Tel.: 91 21 11
Telex: 27821
Cable: UNISANTE Geneva

Fields of activity include health services development; family
health; health manpower; communicable and non-communicable
diseases; therapeutic substances; health statistics; mental health;
and environmental health, including community water supply, sanitation and environmental protection.

The principal opportunities for consulting engineers are in preinvestment studies for water supply and waste water disposal; air,
water, and soil pollution; public health engineering; and training.

Procedure

WHO keeps a general roster of consulting engineers and management firms specializing in water supply, waste management, and water and air pollution control. Interested parties are required to fill out a WHO questionnaire in order to be listed.

Selection Methods

1. WHO reviews its Consultant Registration Files to select a long list of firms based on project needs, a firm qualifications and interest, and acceptability to client.
2. The selection committee makes a short list and clears it with the host government.
3. Short-listed firms are invited to submit proposals.
4. Selection is based on personnel; understanding of the project objectives and requirements; organization and systems for project management; the program proposed for the training of national staff; and the degree of compliance with the terms of reference as well as the justification for any deviations.

The reviewers' reports are submitted to the WHO selection committee, which assesses the proposals and makes recommendations according to order of preference.

The environmental health division then invites the firm with the preferred proposal to negotiate a contract agreement. If those negotiations fail, the second firm of preference is invited for negotiations.

After a contract agreement is signed, WHO normally allows one month for the consultant to mobilize field staff.

The United Nations Industrial Development Organization (UNIDO)

Head
Purchase & Contract Services
United Nations Industrial Development Organization
P.O. Box 300
A-1400 Vienna, Austria
Tel.: 26310
Telex: 135612
Cable: UNIDO Vienna

Fields of activity include industrial planning and programming; feasibility and marketing studies; assistance in establishing pilot plants and industrial estates; and advisory services in industrial sectors such as petro-chemicals.

Procedure

All registered firms are entered in the computer. UNIDO requests registered companies to update their references after three or four years. The agency is in the process of computerizing firms according to their specialties. To be considered for specific projects, expressions of interest are necessary.

Selection Methods

1. UNIDO selects a long list of names from its files. The list must be approved by the government of the country in which the project is to be carried out.
2. Terms of reference and an estimate of man-months necessary to complete the work are presented to a short list of five to ten consultants.
3. Final selection of proposals submitted by consultants is based on a demonstrated grasp of the project aim, the proposed plan of operation, the experience of personnel to be assigned, and price.

UNIDO invites costed proposals, which are analyzed by UNIDO and awarded on the basis of the lowest acceptable proposal. Awards are based primarily on the technical quality of the proposal.

Information on a project is available through the UNIDO Newsletter as well as from the UNDP *Development Forum/Business Edition*.

United Nations Department of Technical Co-operation for Development (UNDTCD)

The Director
Contracts and Procurement Branch Department of Technical Co-operation for Development
United Nations Secretariat
New York, NY 10017
U.S.A.
Tel.: (212) 754-8947
Telex: 232422
Cable: UNATIONS NY

Fields of activity include surveys or feasibility studies for the utilization of mineral, geothermal, surface water, and water resources; transportation studies; power development; aerial photography and mapping; remote sensing; photo interpretation; geological and geophysical surveys; hydrological surveys; flood control; river-basin planning; research and training for urban and regional planning; national and regional economic and social development planning and implementation; public administration and strengthening of government services; oceanographic studies; demographic studies; computer installations and computerization; harbors and ports; and drilling for minerals and groundwater.

Procedure

Registration is necessary. Interested parties must return to the chief of the contracts section a technical data questionnaire and punchcard. The long list is taken from registered consultants expressing interest in a particular project.

1. A short list, normally limited to five or six firms, is submitted to a UN panel and to the recipient country.
2. Terms of reference are established.
3. Letters inviting proposals are sent to those on the short list. Invitations usually ask for costed proposals.
4. The successful bidder is invited to meet with UN staff and negotiate terms.

A firm that has been engaged to help establish the terms of reference for a project is not generally considered for the short list.

United Nations Habitat and Human Settlements Foundation (UNHHSF)

Contracts and Procurement Officer
Administration Section
United Nations Habitat and Human Settlements Foundation
P.O. Box 30030
Nairobi, Kenya
Tel.: 332383
Telex: 22068
Cable: UNIHABITAT Nairobi

Fields of activity include settlement policies and strategies, including the integration of economic, social and physical development plans at national and regional levels; settlement planning, including area development for tourism purposes; shelter, including building materials and construction technology; settlement infrastructure and services, including transportation, waste disposal, water supply, education facilities, health facilities and environmental protection; land requirements for settlements, including land use planning, property legislation and land taxation measures; settlement institutions and management, including legislative, organizational and administrative requirements, and training in human-settlement disciplines; and public participation in settlement development, including organization of cooperatives and self-help programs.

Procedure

Registration is necessary, but as of 1986 UNHHSF did not have standard registration forms. Firms should make general written submissions, which they will be asked to update when a computer program is established.

Selection Methods

1. UNHHSF selects a short list of subcontracting firms from its files, based on demonstrated expertise in the areas covered by the terms of reference of the contract. This list must be approved by the government of the country in which the subcontract is to be carried out.
2. Job specifications are prepared by UNHHSF, together with a schedule of man-months and an estimated budget cost. Firms on the approved short list are invited to submit technical proposals in accordance with these terms.
3. Final selection is made on the basis of the experience of assigned personnel; the firm's record in performing work similar to the project; a demonstrated grasp of project purposes and procedures; the presented work plan; the nature of any proposed joint-venture arrangements; and price.
4. Proposals are analysed by the section concerned, and subcontracts are awarded on the basis of the best technical proposal within the budget limit. Price is only considered as a factor when two acceptable proposals are equal in all other respects.

During execution of subcontracts, UNHHSF monitors the progress of the work through field visits by headquarters technical staff. In the case of large or complex projects, the UNHHSF may assign a senior adviser to the project full-time to give direct technical supervision and provide liaison with government agencies.

The World Bank (WB)

1818 H Street, N.W.
Washington, D.C. 20433
U.S.A.
Tel.: (202) 477-1234
Telex: ITT 440098
      WUB 089650
Cable: INBAFRAD Washington DC

The World Bank is a group of three institutions: the International Bank for Reconstruction and Development (IBRD), the International Development Association (IDA), and the International Finance Corporation (IFC). Owned by the governments of 150 countries, it is the largest source of finance for international work on capital development projects, particularly in the fields of agriculture transportation, energy, and water resources. More recently, emphasis has been placed on urbanization and social development. The current range of technical assistance services to developing countries also includes telecommunications; water supply and sewerage facilities; roads, railways, ports, and airports; industry; mining; tourism; low-cost housing; nutrition; and development banking. The Bank also serves frequently as executing agency for projects financed by the United Nations Development Programme.

Procedure

To assist in the selection of consultants, the Bank maintains a register, "Data on Consulting Firms" (DACON), containing information on forms submitted by consultants. To ensure that only consulting firms capable of undertaking the assignment are invited to submit proposals, the Bank reviews and approves a short list prepared by the borrower. The short list is normally prepared from a longer list obtained by advertising, from the borrower's knowledge, or from expressions of interest submitted by consultants.

For loan projects, which comprise over 90% of the cases in which consulting firms are involved, selection is made by the borrower.

The borrower compiles the short list which is subject to approval by the Bank. The terms of reference are agreed upon by the Bank and the borrower, and the firms on the short list are invited to make proposals. The Bank normally requires contracts to be mutually satisfactory to the Bank, the borrower, and the consultants.

A booklet entitled *Guidelines for the Use of Consultants by World Bank Borrowers and by the World Bank as Executing Agency* is readily obtainable from the Office of Consulting Services Officer at the World Bank.

To fully understand the process of World Bank financing and the selection of consultants for IBRD financed projects, I recommend the publication, *The Project Cycle.* It is available at no charge from the IBRD bookstore in Washington, D.C.

Inter-American Development Bank (IDB)

1300 New York Avenue, N.W.
Washington, D.C. 20057
Tel.: (202) 623-1000
Telex: 089685
Cable: INTAMBANC Washington

The Inter-American Development Bank is an institution of 43 member nations, of which sixteen are countries outside the region.

Its purpose is to accelerate the development of its Latin American and Caribbean countries. The bank has given strong support to the development efforts of the Latin American countries by financing high-priority economic and social development projects in the private and public sectors; providing technical cooperation for research and training activities; and promoting the exchange of information about productive capacity and social welfare. The bank uses its own resources as well as funds mobilized in capital-exporting countries.

Procedure

As soon as a loan project is approved by the Board of Executive Directors, an announcement is made through press releases to public and private entities on the bank's mailing list. A consulting firm should ask to be on the mailing list by contacting the Office of External Relations. The best source of information is the monthly publication of the IDB summary in the UN *Development Forum/ Business Edition.*

The bank maintains a computer-based register of consulting firms which may also be used by its borrowers. The IDB form for the registration of consultants is the same as the World Bank's. The bank must approve the short list of consulting firms (at least three and no more than six) from which a borrower invites unpriced proposals. It must also approve the selection procedure and the terms of reference describing the work to be performed.

Particular projects may include restrictions on the nationalities of consulting firms based on funding sources.

All foreign firms are encouraged (if not required by local law) to make use of local firms or individuals through sub-contracting, joint-venturing or other means. Where a local firm is as well qualified as foreign firms, preference will be given to the local firm.

A 1985 booklet, *Use of Consulting Firms by Inter-American Development Bank and its Borrowers*, is available from the Office of Professional Services Firms at the bank.

Asian Development Bank (AsDB)

P.O. Box 789
Manila
Philippines
Tel.: 831-72-11, 831-72-51
Telex: (RCA) 23103 ADB PH
         (ITT) 40571 ADB PM
         (ETPI) 63587 ADB PN

Capital development projects in Asian countries, from Afghanistan to the Pacific Islands, are funded by the Asian Development Bank. This bank derives its funds from Asian countries as well as from the major industrial countries of the world.

The bank has three projects departments. Agriculture and Rural Development deals with agriculture, rural development, irrigation, fisheries, and livestock. Infrastructure deals with infrastructure projects including airports, highways, ports, railways and telecommunications, water and sewage, urban development, and education. Industry and Development deals with development finance, industry, and power.

The Consulting Services Division comes under the administrative control of the Central Projects Services Office. Inquiries should be addressed to the manager of the Consulting Services Division.

Procedure

Registry proposal review, selection, and contract execution procedures are similar to those of the World Bank. Expressions of interest in loan projects should be addressed to the borrower, with copies directed to the bank. Consultants are in general selected from member countries. Some emphasis is placed on the use of indigenous firms who are encouraged to cooperate with international consultants.

At the time of registration, a personal presentation is recommended.

The booklet, *Uses of Consultants by Asian Development Bank and its Borrowers*, is obtainable from the Consulting Services Division.

African Development Bank (AfDB)

P.O. Box 1387
Abidjan 01 Ivory Coast
Tel.: 320711
Telex: 3717/3263/3498
Cable: AFDEV Abidjan

The African Development Bank funds capital development projects in the sub-Sahara area of Africa, excluding South Africa. Bank projects are directed by the Director of Operations.

Procedure

The procedure in handling projects and retaining consultants is similar to that of the IBRD. Personal contact with government officials in client countries is a definite advantage for placement on the short list. Language ability is also important.

European Development Fund (EDF)

(Administered by the Commission of the
European Communities)
200 Rue de la Loi
B-1040 Brussels Belgium
Tel.: 235 1111
Telex: 21877
Cable: COMEUR BRUSSELS

The European Commission (EC), is the main instrument by which financial and technical aid is channeled from the European Economic Community to the 61 African, Caribbean, and Pacific (ACP) states that have acceded to the Lome Convention. The EC provides financial aid for capital projects; development schemes in agriculture; investments in economic and social infrastructure; and technical assistance of all kinds preceding, accompanying, or following investments. It cooperates with the European Investment Bank and with other suppliers of funds.

Procedure

The Directorate-General for Development (D.G. VIII) of the Commission of the European Communities implements the aid programs. The technical assistance department maintains a register of consultants who are experienced in the kinds of projects financed by the fund. On the basis of the register, D.G. VIII draws up short lists of consultants asked to submit proposals for specific projects. The recipient country chooses the consultant. Application forms for registration, which is automatic, are available from D.G. VIII. For more information, see the brochure, *How to Participate in Contracts Financed by the European Development Fund*, which is available from the Office for Official Publications of the European Communities, P.O. Box 1003, Luxembourg.

Kuwait Fund For Arab Economic Development (KFAED)

P.O. Box 2921
Kuwait, Kuwait
Telex: 22025/22613
Cable: ALSUNDUK

Initially, KFAED activities were limited to Arab countries, but credits are now awarded to non-Arab Muslim and other developing countries. Policies are generally similar to those of the World Bank.

Procedures

The fund expects governments to submit loan applications based on feasibility studies, but it also assists the poorest countries with technical assistance grants for hiring consultants.

Although the fund may make loans for projects in any developing country, Arab countries get first priority, followed by African countries.

Selection of Consultants

From a computerized roster containing approximately 1,200 consultants, the fund prepares a short list which is approved by the borrower. Consultants are generally employed for engineering services such as feasibility studies, design, and supervision rather than turn-key projects.

Arab Fund For Economic And Social Development (AFESD)

P.O. Box 21923
Kuwait
Kuwait
Tel.: 431870
Telex: 22153
Cable: INMARABI Kuwait

The Arab Fund, formed by the twenty-one members of the Arab League, lends only to Arab countries and prefers projects of multinational character. Technical assistance is occasionally granted. Examples of large-scale projects are agricultural development in Sudan and the creation of a telecommunication system among Arab countries.

Selection of Consultants

More than half the borrowing countries prepare short lists and terms of reference, which are approved by the fund. The others (the least developed countries) require the help of the fund. Because the fund is sometimes asked to prepare short lists for projects it does not finance, consultants are advised to stay in contact with the fund as well as with the borrowing countries.

The fund insists on priced proposals, but the selection of consultants is made purely on technical merits. Only when the price is far above the budget is the cost considered. The fund is not in favor of turn-key projects, but wants the consultant to play the conventional role from feasibility study to supervision.

Banque Arabe de Development Economique En Afrique (BADEA)
(Arab Bank for Economic Development in Africa)

> P.O. Box 2640
> Khartoum, The Democratic Republic of the Sudan
> Tel.: 73646/7/8/9
> Telex: 248
> Cable: BADEA Khartoum

The bank is financed by the Arab League. All the member countries of the Arab League, except the two Yemens, Somalia, and Djibouti, are members. The recipient countries are African countries who are not members of the Arab League. The purpose of the bank is to contribute to African economic development by providing all or part of the financing required for economic development projects; promoting and stimulating Arab investment in Africa; and supplying technical assistance to the African countries. In 1976 the Special Arab Aid Fund for Africa (SAAFA) was taken over by BADEA.

The bank normally co-finances with other agencies, especially the World Bank.

Selection of Consultants

The bank normally leaves the selection of consultants to the borrowers or to the co-financers.

Abu Dhabi Fund For Arab Economic Development (ADFAED)

> P.O. Box 814
> Abu Dhabi United Arab Emirates
> Tel.: 22865/6
> Telex: 2287
> Cable: FUND Abu Dhabi

The fund is financed and managed by the Abu Dhabi government. Its objectives are to help Arab, African, and Asian states develop their economies by means of loans; capital support for development projects; and technical aids for survey studies and technical investment.

Selection of Consultants

The ADFAED accepts the DACON (World Bank) registration form. The borrower prepares a short list of consultants to be approved by the fund. The borrower always has the last word in choosing a consultant. Price is always taken into consideration in the choice.

Arab Authority For Agricultural Investment and Development (AAAID)

P.O. Box 2102
Khartoum, The Democratic Republic of the Sudan
Tel.: 72600
Telex: 441
Cable: ISTISMARAB Khartoum

AAAID, generally known as Triple Aid, invests and manages mainly agricultural projects in the Sudan.

Selection of Consultants

AAAID has prepared its own registration form for consultants, using FIDIC's form with the addition of information regarding capability in agriculture. Short lists include no more than five consultants. Consultants are employed to prepare feasibility studies.

Saudi Fund for Development (SFD)

Director, Project Follow-up Department
The Saudi Fund for Development
P.O. Box 1887

Riyadh, Kingdom of Saudi Arabia
Tel.: 4640292
Telex: 201145/201744
Cable: SUNDOQ SJ

The Saudi Fund for Development provides loans to developing countries for projects in agriculture, infrastructure, health, and education. Projects are funded in countries in Asia, Africa, Europe, and South America.

Selection of Consultants

The fund has started registration for consultants.

The agency helps borrowers by preparing a short list of consultants and also evaluates consultants who submit proposals. Technical and financial proposals are submitted together. The firms are judged mainly on technical proposals. Financial proposals should be reasonable and in line with the services offered. A ranking list of two or three firms is prepared. Negotiations are conducted with the first-ranked firm. Should these fail, the next firm is approached.

Fixed fees are sometimes paid, but payment is usually cost plus a fixed fee, with a ceiling estimate.

The fund does not fund turn-key projects. Firms are not required to form associations with local consulting firms.

Islamic Development Bank

P.O. Box 5925
Jeddah, Kingdom of Saudi Arabia
Tel.: 636 0329
Telex: 401147/2

All countries who are members of the Islamic Secretariat qualify for membership in the bank. The Operations and Projects Department handles project work and deals with consultants.

Procedure

The purpose of the bank is to foster the economic development and social progress of its members through loans, equity, or leasing in public or private enterprises.

Selection of Consultants

Borrowers submit short lists of consultants to the bank for approval. The two-envelope system has been adopted, with the requirement that costs be outlined in detail.

The bank registration form is similar to the FIDIC form.

The agreement between borrower and consultant is reviewed by the bank. Fees are normally based on a fixed rate for man-months, plus reimbursable costs, within an established limit.

Caribbean Development Bank (CDB)

P.O. Box 408
Barbados, West Indies
St. Michael
Tel.: 61152
Telex: WB 2287
Cable: CARIBANKD Barbados

The Caribbean Development Bank lends money for comparatively small projects in agriculture, tourism, infrastructure, and manufacturing industries.

Procedure

The Caribbean Development Bank maintains a register of firms. Where fees and expenses are estimated to exceed US$ 50,000, all opportunities for consultants are advertised. Where fees and expenses are estimated to be less than US$ 50,000, a short list is prepared. Consultants are selected by borrowers, subject to the approval of the bank. The cost of services is usually requested with proposals.

Central American Bank For Economic Integration (CABEI)

Banco Centroamericano de Integracion Economica
Apartado Postal 772
Tegucigalpa, D.C. Honduras

The CABEI is a regional institution for operations in the Organization of Central American Countries.

The back finances feasibility studies for capital projects and investments, as well as technical assistance programs.

Procedure

Loans to member countries, private enterprise, government, and decentralized organizations and institutions are approved by the directors of the bank.

The bank must approve selection procedures and terms of reference describing the work to be performed. Proposals are requested through press releases.

According to the source of funds for specific projects, there may be restrictions on the nationalities of consulting firms to be engaged.

The bank encourages participation by Central American consultants and consulting firms. Whenever possible, preference is given to regional firms.

Agency for International Development (AID)

AID finances limited-assistance programs in agriculture and food production, with emphasis on nutrition; human resources; population control; health care; and low-cost education. Research and pilot programs receive priority. Many AID programs are implemented through grants to U.S. universities and nonprofit organizations rather than independent consultants in private practice. AID also funds capital projects in a number of countries (such as Jordan, Egypt, and Pakistan), selecting consultants directly in some cases, and allowing host-country agencies to choose and appoint consulting firms in others. Policy statements and outlines of activities can be obtained directly from the U.S. Department of State.

Export-Import Bank of the United States (EX-IM BANK)

811 Vermont Ave., N.W.
Washington, D.C. 20571
Tel.: (202) 566-2117
Hotline: (800) 424-5201
Telex: 98-461

The Eximbank is an independent U.S. government agency that helps finance the export of U.S. goods and services. Although the Eximbank rarely employs consultants directly, American citizens and U.S. firms benefit from its activities. These include assuming the risks involved in financing the production and sale of export goods; financing foreign buyers of U.S. goods and services; and matching foreign credit competition. The Eximbank extends working-capital guarantees; medium-term guarantees; medium-term credits; small-business credits; engineering-multiplier programs; direct loans; and financial guarantees.

Private Export Funding Corporation (PEFCO)

> 280 Park Avenue
> New York, NY 10017
> Tel.: (212) 557-3100

The Private Export Funding Corporation (PEFCO) serves as a supplemental source of long-term financing for foreign buyers of U.S. exports. A private corporation owned by a group of 55 banks and several industrial corporations, PEFCO works closely with the Export-Import Bank in offering direct loans of long maturity at fixed interest rates. The minimum loan is US$ 1 million and the maximum maturity is five years.

Although PEFCO rarely uses consultant services, PEFCO-financed projects can provide significant opportunities for U.S. consulting firms.

Foreign Credit Insurance Association (FCIA)

> 40 Rector Street
> 11th Floor
> New York, NY 10006
> Tel.: (212) 306-5000

The Foreign Credit Insurance Association protects U.S. exporters against loss when foreign customers default for political or commercial reasons.

FCIA indirectly serves U.S. consultants by providing insurance at reasonable rates. Individuals and firms can therefore seek engagements in markets where the risks would not normally be covered by standard policies.

United States Trade And Development Program (TDP)

U.S. International Development Corporation Agency
Washington, DC 20523

This government agency finances planning services for development projects that lead to the export of U.S. goods and services. Recipient countries pay the full cost of project implementation.

TDP is involved in a wide range of public sector and private investor projects in energy, industry, infrastructure, and agribusiness. TDP emphasizes development activities pertaining to strategic minerals and metals. The agency uses the services of contracts with U.S. consultants and U.S. consulting firms.

Appendices

Appendix A

CHECKLIST OF SOVEREIGN NATIONS OF THE WORLD

Country	Primary Languages	Capital	Year of Independence
Afghanistan	Pushtu, Dari	Kabul	1921
Albania	Albanian	Tirana	1918
Algeria	Arabic, French	Algiers	1962
American Samoa	English, Samoan	Pago Pago	n.a.
Angola	Portuguese	Luanda	1975
Antigua and Barbuda	English	St. Johns	n.a.
Argentina	Spanish	Buenos Aires	1816
Australia	English	Canberra	1901
Austria	German	Vienna	
Bahamas	English	Nassau	1973
Bahrain	Arabic	Manama	1971
Bangladesh	Bengali, English	Dacca	1971
Barbados	English	Bridgetown	1966
Belgium	French, Flemish	Brussels	1839
Belize	English, Mayan, Spanish	Belmopan	1981
Benin	French	Porto Novo	1960

Country	Primary Languages	Capital	Year of Independence
Bermuda	English	Hamilton	n.a.
Bhutan	Bhutanese	Thimbu	1971
Bolivia	Spanish	La Paz, Sucre	1825
Botswana	English, Setswana	Gaborone	1966
Brazil	Portuguese	Brasilia	1822
Brunei	Malay, English, Chinese	Bandor Seri Begawan	1984
Bulgaria	Bulgarian	Sofia	1878
Burkina Faso	French	Ouagadougou	1960
Burma	Burmese	Rangoon	1948
Burundi	French	Mujumbura	1962
Cameroon	French, English	Yaounde	1960/61
Canada	English	Ottawa	1867
Cape Verde	Portuguese, Crioulo	Praia	1975
Central African Rep.	French	Bangui	1960
Chad	French	Njamena	1960
Chile	Spanish	Santiago	1818
Colombia	Spanish	Bogota	1819
Comoros	Shaafi Islam, French	Moroni	1975
Congo, People's Rep.	French	Brazzaville	1960
Costa Rica	Spanish	San Jose	1821

Country	Language(s)	Capital	Year
Cuba	Spanish	Havana	1902
Cyprus	Greek, Turkish	Nicosia	1960
Czechoslovakia	Czech, Slovak	Prague	1918
Denmark	Danish	Copenhagen	
Djibouti	French, Somali, Arabic	Djibouti	1977
Dominica	English, French	Roseau	1978
Dominican Rep.	Spanish	Santo Domingo	1844
Ecuador	Spanish	Quito	1830
Egypt, Arab Rep.	Arabic	Cairo	1952
El Salvador	Spanish	San Salvador	1821
Equatorial Guinea	Spanish	Malabo	1968
Ethiopia	Amharic, English	Addis Ababa	
Fiji	English	Suva	1970
Finland	Finnish	Helsinki	1917
France	French	Paris	n.a.
French Guiana	French	Cayenne	n.a.
Gabon	French	Libreville	1960
Gambia, The	English	Banjul	1965
German Dem. Rep.	German	East Berlin	1945
Germany, Fed. Rep.	German	Bonn (Berlin)	1945
Ghana	English	Accra	1957
Greece	Greek	Athens	1830
Greenland	Nuuk	Godthad	n.a.

Country	Primary Languages	Capital	Year of Independence
Grenada	English	St. George's	1974
Guadeloupe	French	Basse Terre	n.a.
Guam	English	Agana	n.a.
Guatemala	Spanish	Guatemala City	1821
Guinea	French	Conakry	1858
Guinea-Bissau	Portuguese	Bissau	1974
Guyana	English	Georgetown	1966
Haiti	French	Port-au-Prince	1804
Honduras	Spanish	Tegucigalpa	1821
Hong Kong	English, Catonese	Victoria	n.a.
Hungary	Hungarian	Budapest	1918
Iceland	Icelandic, English	Reykjavik	n.a.
India	Hindi, English	New Delhi	1947
Indonesia	Bahasa Indonesia	Djakarta	1949
Iran. Islamic Rep.	Persian (Farsi)	Tehran	n.a.
Iraq	Arabic, Kurdish	Baghdad	1932
Ireland	Irish, English	Dublin	1921
Israel	Hebrew, Arabic	Jerusalem (Tel-Aviv)	1948
Italy	Italian	Rome	1861
Ivory Coast	French	Abidjan	1960
Jamaica	English	Kingston	1962

Japan	Japanese	Tokyo	n.a.
Jordan	Arabic	Amman	1946
Kampuchea, Dem.	Khmer	Phnom	n.a.
Kenya	Kiswahili, English	Nairobi	1963
Kiribati	English	Tarawa	1079
Korea, Dem. People's Rep.	Korean	Pyongyang	1948
Korea, Rep. of	Korean	Seoul	1948
Kuwait	Arabic	Kuwait	1961
Lao PDR	Lao	Vientiane	1954
Lebanon	Arabic	Beirut	1941
Lesotho	English, Sesotho	Maseru	1966
Liberia	English	Monrovia	1847
Libya	Arabic	Tripoli	1951
Luxembourg	French	Luxembourg	1839
Macao	Portuguese	Macau	n.a.
Madagascar	Malayasy, French	Antananarivo	1960
Malawi	English, Chichewa	Lilongwe	1964
Malaysia	Malay, English	Kuala Lumpur	1963
Maldives	Kiheci	Male'	1965
Mali	French	Bamako	1960
Malta	English	Malta	1964
Martinique	French, Creole	Fort-de-France	n.a.
	French		
Mauritania	French	Nouakchott	1960

Country	Primary Languages	Capital	Year of Independence
Mauritius	English	Port Louis	1968
Mexico	Spanish	Mexico City	1821
Mongolia	Mongolian	Ulan Bator	n.a.
Montserrat	English	Plymouth	n.a.
Morocco	Arabic	Rabat	1956
Mozambique	Portuguese	Laurenco Marques	1975
Nambia	Afrikaans	Windhoek	(UN Trust)
Nepal	Nepali	Katmandu	1923
Netherlands	Dutch	The Hague	1814
Netherlands Antilles	Dutch, English, Spanish	Willemstad	n.a.
New Caledonia	French	Noumea	n.a.
New Zealand	English	Wellington	1907
Nicaragua	Spanish	Managua	1821
Niger	French	Niamey	1960
Nigeria	English	Lagos	1960
Norway	Norwegian	Oslo	1905
Oman	Arabic	Masqat	1971
Pacific Islands, Trust Ter.	English	Saipan	n.a.
Pakistan	Urdu, English	Islamabad	1947
Panama	Spanish	Panama City	1903

Papua New Guinea	English	Port Moresby	1974
Paraguay	Spanish	Asuncion	1811
Peru	Spanish	Lima	1821
Philippines	Filipino, English, Spanish	Quezon City (Manila)	1946
Poland	Polish	Warsaw	n.a.
Portugal	Portuguese	Lisbon	1910
Puerto Rico	Spanish, English	San Juan	n.a.
Qatar	Arabic	Doha	1971
Romania	Romanian	Bucharest	1878
Rwanda	French, Kinyarwanda	Kigali	1962
St. Christopher & Nevis	English	Basseterre	1983
St. Lucia	English, French	Castries	1979
St. Vincent	English	Kingstown	n.a.
Sao Tome and Principe	Portuguese	Sao Tome	1975
Saudi Arabia	Arabic	Riyadh	1902
Senegal	French	Dakar	1960
Seychelles	Creole, English, French	Victoria	1976
Sierre Leone	English	Freetown	1961
Singapore	Chinese (Mandarin), Malay, Tamil, English	Singapore	1960
Solomon Islands	English	Honiara	1978
Somalia	Arabic, Italian, French	Mogadishu	1960

Country	Primary Languages	Capital	Year of Independence
South Africa	English, Afrikaans	Pretoria, Capetown	1961
Spain	Spanish	Madrid	n.a.
Sri Lanka	Sinhala	Colombo	1948
Sudan	Arabic	Khartoum	1956
Suriname	Dutch	Paramaribo	1975
Swaziland	SiSwati, English	Mbabane	1968
Sweden	Swedish	Stockholm	n.a.
Switzerland	German, French, Italian	Bern	n.a.
Syrian Arab Rep.	Arabic	Damascus	1946
Tanzania	Swahili, English	Dar-es-Salaam	1961
Thailand	Thai	Bangkok	n.a.
Togo	French	Lone	1960
Tonga	English	Nuku'alofa	1970
Trinidad and Tobago	English	Port-of-Spain	1962
Tunisia	Arabic, French	Tunis	1956
Turkey	Turkish	Ankara	1923
Tuvalu	English	Funafuti	1978
U.S.S.R.	Russian	Moscow	n.a.
Uganda	English, Kiswahili	Kampala	1962
United Arab Emirates	Arabic	Abu Dhabi	1971

United Kingdom	English, Welsh, Gaelic	London	n.a.
United States	English	Washington, D.C.	1776
Uruguay	Spanish	Montevideo	1825
Vanuatu	English	Port Vila	1980
Venezuela	Spanish	Caracas	1830
Vietnam	Vietnamese, French	Hanoi	1975
Virgin Islands (U.S.)	English, Spanish, Creole	Charlotte Amalie	n.a.
Western Samoa	English, Samoan	Apia	1962
Yemen Arab Rep.	Arabic	Sana	1962
Yemen, PDR	Arabic	Aden	1967
Yugoslavia	Serbo, Croat	Belgrade	1918
Zaire	French	Kinshasha	1960
Zambia	French	Lusaka	1960
Zimbabwe	English, Shona, Ndebele	Salibsury	1980

Appendix B

FOREIGN CHAMBERS OF COMMERCE AND ASSOCIATIONS IN THE UNITED STATES

Africa

African-American Chamber
of Commerce, Inc.
200 Madison Avenue
New York, NY 10016
212/561-2025

Argentina

Argentine-American Chamber
of Commerce
50 West 34th St., 6th Fl.
Room C2
New York, NY 10001
212/564-3855

Austria

U.S.-Austrian Chamber of
Commerce, Inc.
165 West 46th Streeet
New York, NY 10036
212/819-0117

Belgium

Belgian-American Chamber of
Commerce in the U.S., Inc.
Suite 1003/1005
50 Rockefeller Plaza
New York, NY 10020
212/247-7613

Brazil

Brazilian-American Chamber
of Commerce, Inc.
Room 610
22 West 48th Street
New York, NY 10036
212/575-9030

Brazilian-American Chamber
of Commerce
1451 Brickell Avenue
Miami, FL 33131
305/377-6700

Brazil California Trade Association
Suite 226
350 South Figueroa Street
Los Angeles, CA 90071
213/627-0634

Chile

North American-Chilean Chamber of
Commerce, Inc.
220 East 81st Street
New York, NY 10028
212/228-5691

China

Chinese Chamber of Commerce of
New York
Room C03
Confucius Plaza
33rd Bowery
New York, NY 10002
212/226-2795

Chinese Chamber of Commerce of
San Francisco
730 Sacramento Street
San Francisco, CA 94108
415/982-3000

Colombia

Colombian-American Association, Inc.
Room 1110
115 Broadway
New York, NY 10006
212/233-7776

Coosta Rica

Costa Rica Export & Investment
  Promotion Center
Suite 400
200 S.E. First Street
Miami, FL 33131
305/358-1891

Dominican Republic

Dominican Republic Export
  Promotion Center
Room 86065
One World Trade Center
New York, NY 10048
212/432-9498

Ecuador

Ecuadorean-American Association,
  Inc.
Room 1110
115 Broadway
New York, NY 10006
212/233-7776

Far East

Far East-America Council of
  Commerce and Industry, Inc.
475 Park Avenue South, 30th Fl.
New York, NY 10016
212/683-4677

Finland

The Finnish-American Chamber
  of Commerce
Fifteenth Floor
540 Madison Avenue
New York, NY 10022
212/832-2588

The Finnish-American Chamber
  of Commerce of the Midwest
Suite 1900
35 East Wacker Drive
Chicago, IL 60601
312/346-1150

France

French-American Chamber of
  Commerce in the U.S.
1350 Avenue of the Americas
New York, NY 10019
212/581-4554

Germany

German-American Chamber of
  Commerce, Inc.
666 Fifth Avenue
New York, NY 10103
212/974-8830

German-American Chamber of
  Commerce of Chicago
77 East Monroe Street
Chicago, IL 60603
312/782-8557

German-American Chamber of
  Commerce of Los Angeles, Inc.
Suite 2212
One Park Plaza Building
3250 Wilshire Boulevard
Los Angeles, CA 90010
213/381-2236

German-American Chamber of
  Commerce of the Pacific Coast, Inc.
Suite 910
465 California Street
San Francisco, CA 94104
415/392-2262

German-American Chamber of
  Commerce
One Farragut Square South
Washington, DC 20006
202/347-0247

Greece

Hellenic-American Chamber of
  Commerce
Room 1508
29 Broadway
New York, NY 10006
212/943-8594

India

India Chamber of Commerce of America
445 Park Avenue
New York, NY 10022
212/755-7181

India-American Chamber of Commerce
P.O. Box 64217
Los Angeles, CA 90064
213/826-3512

Indo-American Chamber of Commerce
c/o The Bank of India
10 South La Salle Street
Chicago, IL 60603
312/621-1200

Indonesia

American-Indonesian Chamber of
Commerce, Inc.
2 Park Avenue
New York, NY 10016
212/683-6170

Ireland

Ireland-United States Council for
Commerce and Industry, Inc.
460 Park Avenue
New York, NY 10022
212/751-2660

Israel

American-Israel Chamber of Commerce
and Industry, Inc.
Room 5416
500 Fifth Avenue
New York, NY 10036
212/354-6510

American-Israel Chamber of Commerce
and Industry, Inc.
ATTN: Max Ratner
Cleveland Center
10800 Brookpark Road
Cleveland, OH 44130
216/267-1200

American-Israel Chamber of Commerce
and Industry, Inc.
Midwest Chapter
180 N. Michigan Avenue
Suite 911
Chicago, IL 60601
312/641-2937

Western States Chamber of Commerce
with Israel
Suite 806
6399 Wilshire Boulevard
Los Angeles, CA 90048
213/658-7910

Italy

Italian Chamber of Commerce of
Chicago
126 West Grand Avenue
Chicago, IL 60610
312/661-1336

Italy-American Chamber of Commerce,
Inc.
Suite 3015
350 Fifth Avenue
New York, NY 10118
212/279-5520

Japan

Honolulu Japanese Chamber of
Commerce
2454 South Beretania Street
Nonlulu, HI 96826
808/949-5531

Japan Business Association of Southern
California
350 S. Figueroa Street
Los Angeles, CA 90071
213/628-1263

Japanese Chamber of Commerce and
Industry of Chicago
Room 2108
230 N. Michigan Avenue
Chicago, IL 60601
312/332-6199

Japanese Chamber of Commerce of
  New York, Inc.
145 West 57th Street
New York, NY 10019
212/246-9774

Japanese Chamber of Commerce of
  Northern California
Room 408
World Affairs Center
312 Sutter Street
San Francisco, CA 94108
415/986-6140

Japanese Chamber of Commerce of
  Southern California
244 S. San Pedro Street
Room 504
Los Angeles, CA 90012
213/626-3067

Korea

Korean Chamber of Commerce
981 S. Western Avenue #201
Los Angeles, CA 90006
213/733-4410

U.S.-Korea Economic Council
555 Lake Avenue
Professional Building
St. James, NY 11780
212/662-8610

Latin America

Chamber of Commerce of
  Latin America in the U.S., Inc.
Suite 3549
One World Trade Center
New York, NY 10048
212/432-9313

Latin Chamber of Commerce
1417 West Flagler Street
Miami, FL 33135
305/642-3870

Latin American Chamber of
  Commerce of Oregon
824 S.W. 5th Avenue
Portland, OR 97204
503/221-1283

Latin American Manufacturing
  Association
901 E. Capitol Street, S.E.
Washington, D.C. 20003
202/546-3803

Pan American Chamber of Commerce
  and Trade Council
Business Information Center
315 Twelfth Avenue
San Francisco, CA 94118
415/752-4093

Pan American Society of the U.S., Inc.
680 Park Avenue
New York, NY 10021
212/744-6868

Lebanon

United States-Lebanese Chamber of
  Commerce
Suite 1345
One World Trade Center
New York, NY 10048
212/432-1133

Mexico

Mexican-American Chamber of
  Commerce of Chicago
3624 W. 26th Street
Chicago, IL 60623
312/762-5662

Mexican-American Chamber of
  Commerce of Arizona
1500 E. Maryland Avenue
Phoenix, AZ 85014
602/252-6448

Mexican Chamber of Commerce of
  The County of Los Angeles
Room 404
125 Paseo de La Plaza
Los Angeles, CA 90012
213/688-7330

The Mexican Chamber of Commerce
  of the U.S., Inc.
233 Broadway
The Woolworth Building, Suite 704
New York, NY 10038
212/227-9171

Mexican Institute for Foreign Trade
Fourth Floor
115 E. 57th Street
New York, NY 10022
212/371-3823

United States-Mexico Chamber of
  Commerce
1000 Potomac Street, NW #102
Washington, D.C. 20007
202/296-5198

U.S.-Mexico Quadripartite Comm.
Center for Inter-American Relations
ATTN: Mr. Roger Stone
680 Park Avenue
New York, NY 10021
212/249-8950

Middle East

American-Arab Association
  Commerce & Industry
Suite 1060
342 Madison Avenue
New York, NY 10017
212/986-7229

Southwest U.S.-Arab Chamber
  of Commerce
319 World Trade Building
Houston, TX 77002
713/222-6152

MidAmerica-Arab Chamber of
  Commerce, Inc.
Suite 2050
135 South LaSalle Street
Chicago, IL 60603
312/782-4654

U.S.-Arab Chamber of Commerce
  (Pacific), Inc.
Suite 920
433 California Street
San Francisco, CA 94104
415/397-5663

U.S.-Arab Chamber of Commerce
Suite 4657
One World Trade Center
New York, NY 10048
212/432-0655

U.S.-Arab Chamber of Commerce
  (Washington Chapter)
Suite 812
1625 Eye Street, N.W.
Washington, D.C. 20006
202/293-3162

The Netherlands

The Netherlands Chamber of
Commerce
  in the U.S., Inc.
Eleventh Floor
One Rockefeller Plaza
New York, NY 10020
212/265-6460

Nigeria

Nigerian-American Chamber of
  Commerce, Inc.
200 Madison Avenue
Third Floor
New York, NY 10016
212/561-2025

Norway

Norwegian-American Chamber of
  Commerce, Inc.
Suite 1908
Midwest Chicago Chapter
360 N. Michigan Avenue
Chicago, IL 60601
312/782-7750

The Norwegian-American Chamber of
  Commerce, Inc.
Suite 360
World Trade Center
350 S. Figueroa Street
Los Angeles, CA 90071
213/626-0338

Norwegian-American Chamber of
  Commerce, Inc.
Upper Midwest Chapter
800 Foshay Tower
Minneapolis, MN 55402
612/332-3338

The Norwegian-American Chamber of
  Commerce, Inc.
800 Third Avenue
New York, NY 10022
212/421-9210

Norwegian-American Chamber of
  Commerce, Inc.
2727 Rainier Bank Tower
Seattle, WA 98101
206/682-5250

Norwegian-American Chamber of
  Commerce, Inc.
Suite 2609
One Embarcadero Center
San Francisco, CA 94111
415/986-0766

Pakistan

U.S. Pakistan-Economic Council
Professional Building
555 Lake Avenue
St. James New York 11780
212/662-8610

Peru

Peruvian-American Association
50 West 34th Street
6th Floor, Suite C2
New York, NY 10001
212/564-3855

The Philippines

The Philippine-American Chamber of
  Commerce, Inc.
Room 809
565 Fifth Avenue
New York, NY 10017
212/972-9326

Philippine-American Chamber of
  Commerce
c/o Philippine Consulate
447 Sutter Street
San Francisco, CA 94108
415/433-6666

Puerto Rico

Puerto Rico Chamber of Commerce
  in the U.S.
200 Madison Avenue
New York, NY 10016
212/561-2028

Spain

Spain-U.S. Chamber of Commerce
Room 4220
500 Fifth Avenue
New York, NY 10110
212/354-7848

Commercial Office of Spain
Suite 946
World Trade Center
350 S. Figueroa Street
Los Angeles, CA 90071
213/628-1406

Sweden

Swedish-American Chamber of
  Commerce, Inc.
One Dag Hammarshjold Plaza
New York, NY 10017
212/838-5530

Swedish-American Chamber of
  Commerce of the Western U.S., Inc.
Suite 268
Ferry Building
World Trade Center
San Francisco, CA 94111
415/781-4188

Trinidad

Trinidad and Tobago Chamber of
  Commerce of the U.S.A., Inc.
c/o Trinidad and Tobago Oil Company
Room 400
1270 Avenue of the Americas
New York, NY 10020
212/541-4615

United Kingdom

British-American Chamber of Commerce
Room 1714
275 Madison Avenue
New York, NY 10016
212/889-0680

British-American Chamber of
  Commerce
3150 California Street
San Francisco, CA 94115
415/567-6128

British-American Chamber of Commerce
  and Trade Center of the Pacific
  Southwest
Suite 224
1640 5th Street
Santa Monica, CA 90401
213/394-4977

Venezuela

The Venezuelan-American Assocation
  of the U.S., Inc.
Room 1110
115 Broadway
New York, NY 10006
212/233-7776

Appendix C

AMERICAN CHAMBERS OF COMMERCE ABROAD

Argentina

Federico Dodds
President
Union Carbide Carbide Argentina
S.A.I.C.S.
Virrey Loreto 2477/81
1426 Buenos Aires, Argentina
Phone: 782-6016
Telex: 21517 CIARG AR
Cable: UNICARBINE BAIRES

Australia

Joseph D. (Joe) Berrier, Jr.
President
American Chamber of Commerce
in Australia
3rd Floor, 50 Pitt Street
Sydney, N.S.W. 2000, Australia
Phone: 241-1907
Telex: 22792 Lincoln
Cable: AMCHAM SYDNEY

Austria

Dr. Elemer T. Balogh
President
The American Chamber of Commerce
in Austria
Turkenstrasse 9
A-1090 Vienna, Austria
Phone: 31-57-51
Telex: 134206 (Attn: Mrs. Bacher)

Belgium

John E. Egbers
Managing Director
Du Pont de Nemours (Belgium)
rue de la Fusee 100
1130 Brussels, Belgium
Phone: 02/722.06.11
Telex: 62788

Bolivia

Charles Bruce
President
The Anschutz Corp.
P.O. Box 1603
La Paz, Bolivia
Phone: 35-55-74
Telex: 2544 METALTR BV
Cable: METRASEA

Brazil, Rio De Janeiro

John P. Polychron
Director President
R.J. Reynolds Tobacos do Brasil, Ltda.
Praia de Botafogo, 440/25
P.O. Box 3588
22.250 Rio de Janeiro, RJ–Brazil
Phone: 286-6162
Telex: 2123539 RJRT BR
Cable: REYNOTABA

Branch Office

David Marler Ferrell
President
American Chamber of Commerce
for Brazil–Salvador
c/o Econtrading S.A.
P.O. Box 596
40.000 Salvador, Bahia, Brazil
Phone: 244-2912, 233-2067

Brazil, Sao Paulo

Enrique Sosa
Director President
Empresas Dow
Caixa Postal 30037
01051, Sao Paolo, SP–Brazil
Phone: 212-1122
Telex: 1122162 DOWQ BR
Cable: DOWINTAL

Chile

Mr. M. Wayne Sandvig
Director
Fundacion Chile
Casilla 773
Santiago, Chile
Phone: 28-16-46
Telex: 0239 FUND CZ

China–PRC

Sally A. Harpole
Graham & James
Jian Guo Hotel, Room 140
Jian Guo Men Wai
Beijing, People's Republic of
    China
Telex: 22439 JGHBJ Cn

Colombia

William Wilde
Chairman of the Board
Fiberglass Colombia S.A.
Apartade Aereo 91932
Bogota, Colombia
Phone: 255-7900
Telex: 44483

Branch Office

Richard Lee
General Manager
Goodyear de Colombia
Apartado Aereo 142
Cali, Valle, Colombia
Phone: 686-141, 689-868
Telex: 55589

Costa Rica

Federico A. Golcher
Managing Partner
Peat, Marwick, Mitchell & Co.
Apartado 10208
1000 San Jose, Costa Rica
Phone: 21-52-22
Telex: 2818 VERIT CR
Cable: VERITATEM

Dominican Republic

Jaak R. Rannik
President
Baez & Rannik, S.A.
P.O. Box 1221
Santo Domingo, Dominican Republic
Phone: 565-6661
Telex: 0034 TATEM DR

Ecuador

Robert L. Rice
General Manager
Xerox del Ecuador, S.A.
P.O. Box 174-A
Quito, Ecuador
Phone: 245-229, 451-614
Telex: 2325 XDOR ED

Ecuador–Guayaquil

Carson Watson
Managing Director
Johnson & Johnson del Ecuador
Casilla 7206
Guayaquil, Ecuador
Phone 39 96 00
Telex: 3396 JANDJE ED

Egypt

Sam Zavatti
President
American Chamber of Commerce
    in Egypt
Cairo Marriott Hotel, Suite 1537
P.O. Box 33 Zamalek
Cairo, Egypt
Phone: 650840/1
Telex: 93464/5 Mar Un

El Salvador

Ramsey L. Moore
President
Moore Commercial S.A. de C.V.
29 Avenida Sur 817
P.O. Box 480
San Salvador, El Salvador
Phone: 71-1200
Telex: 20238 MOORE

France

John Crawford
Partner
Surrey & Morse
53, avenue Montaigne
75008 Paris, France
Phone: (1) 359-2349

Germany

Frederick G. Drake
President
General Electric–Deutchland
Praunheimer Landstr. 50
6000 Frankfurt 90
Germany
Phone: 069-7607-325/6
Telex: 412 002

Greece

Charles J. Politis
President
APCO Industries S.A.
Group Corporate Offices
18 Academias Street
Athens 134, Greece
Phone: 3618-008
Telex: 212404 APCO GR

Demetre N. Petsiavas
General Manager
Petsiavas N., A.E.
11 Nicodemon & Voulis Streets
Athens 119, Greece
Phone: 323.0451
Cable: KEMTEX
Telex: 21.5983 Npsa Gr

Guatemala

Spencer Manners
Vice President, Latin American
Operations
Foodpro International, Inc.
12 Calle 1-25, No. 1114
P.O. Box 89-A, Zona 10
Guatemala City, Guatemala
Phone: 320-490
Telex: 5743

Haiti

Robert L. Burgess
General Manager
Sylvania Overseas Trading Corporation
P.O. Box 1005
Port-au-Prince, Haiti
Phone: 6-0037, 6-3859
Telex: 2030232
Cable: SOTC

Honduras

J. Mark Werner
Attorney-at-Law
21 Ave. S.O. 9 y 10
C. #88 Colonia Trejo
P.O. Box 500
San Pedro Sula, Honduras
Phone: 54-27-43, 54-42-58
Telex: 5693

Hong Kong

Gage McAfee
Coudert Brothers
32/F, Alexandra House
3105 Alexandra House
16 Chater Road, Central
Hong Kong
Phone: 5-26595

Indonesia

Harvey Goldstein
Executive Vice President
P.T. Resources Management
    Indonesia
J1. Melawai VI/8
Kebayoran Baru
Jakarta Selatan, Indonesia

Ireland

A.J. Fox, Jr.
Managing Director
Union Camp Ireland
Ashbourne
County Meath, Ireland
Phone: 350411
Telex: 31187 UCIL

Israel

Mr. Arik Makleff
President
Israel-America Chamber of Commerce
Dexter Chemical (International) Ltd.
P.O. Box 300
Yavne 70652
Israel
Phone: (08) 437011
Telex: 341907 OXCEM IL

Italy

Michael N. Bitas
Senior Partner
Peat, Marwick, Mitchell & Co.
Piazza Meda 3
20121 Milano, Italy
Phone: (02) 77.351
Telex: 312604 PMM1

Japan

Herbert F. Hayde
Chairman
Burroughs Company Ltd.
13-1, Shimomiyabicho
Shinjuku-ku
Tokyo 162, Japan
Phone: 03-235-3337
Telex: 232278 BURTOK J

Japan–Okinawa

Murray V. Harlan
President
The American Chamber of Commerce
    in Okinawa
P.O. Box 235, Koza
Okinawa City, 904, Japan
Phone: 098945-4558
Telex: J79873 Nansei Ok
Cable: AMCHAM OKINAWA

Korea

James H. Riddle
Vice President
Teledyne
Room 303, Namsong Mansion
260-199, Itaewon-dong
Yongan-gu, Seoul, Korea

Malaysia

Russell A. Klingler
Vice President
American International Assurance Ltd.
AIA Building
P.O. Box 759
Kuala Lumpur, Malaysia

Mexico

Purdy C. Jordan
Director
Embotelladora Tarahumara, S.A. de
C.V.
Rio Amazonas No. 43
06500 Mexico, D.F. Mexico
Phone: 591-0066
Telex: 1775481 CCDFME

Branch Offices

James Despain
Managing Director
Conek, S.A. de C.V.
Apartado Postal 2781
Monterrey, Nuevo Leon, Mexico

Branch Office

Adolf B. Horn, Jr.
Managing Director
Helados Bing, S.A.
Apdo. 31-72
45070 Guadalajara, Jalisco, Mexico
Phone: 15-88-22

Morocco

Jean-Pierre Bernex
General Manager
Colgate Palmolive Maroc
11 Avenue des Forces Armees Royales
Casablanca, Morocco

The Netherlands

Sig E. Von Kutzleben
Managing Director
Fluor Nederland B.V.
c/o The American Chamber of
    Commerce in the Netherlands
2517 KJ The Hague, The Netherlands
Phone: 023-339020
Telex: 41219

New Zealand

Maurice P. Boland
Director
3M New Zealand Ltd.
P.O. Box 33-246, Takapuna
Auckland 9, New Zealand
Phone: 444-4760
Telex: NZ 2601

Nicaragua

Julio Vigil
President
Vigil y Caligaris
Apartado 202
Managua, Nicaragua
Phone: 262-491
Telex: 1255 VIGIL

Pakistan

Hasan I. Kazmi
President
American Business Council of
    Pakistan
3rd Floor, Shaheen Commercial
    Complex
M.R. Kayani Road, GPO Box 1322
Karachi, Pakistan
Phone: 526436
Telex: 25620 CHASE PK

Panama

Robert M. Cooney
Vice President
Citibank, N.A.
Apartado 555
Paname 9A, Republica de Panama
Phone: 64-4044, 64-1255
Telex: 2129 TRT

Paraguay

Desiderio Enciso
Director
Petroleos Paraguayos
Chile y Oliva, Piso 4
Asuncion, Paraguay
Telex: 5153 PETROPAR

Peru

Miguel J. Godoy
President
M.J. Godoy & Co., S.A.
P.O. Box 5661
Lima 100, Peru
Phone: 28-7006, 28-7515
Telex: 20454 MIGOYCO
Cable: MIGOYCO

Philippines

A. Lewis Burridge
President
Sterling Asia
8th Floor, Teza Towers
Herrera Corner Alfaro Streets
Salcedo Village, Makati, Metro Manila
Philippines
Phone: 815-9526
Telex: 22531

Portugal

Robert R. Langelier
Director Gerente General
General Motors de Portugal
Av Marcechal Gomes de Costa 33
1800 Lisboa, Portugal
Phone: 853996
Telex: 12599 Autorex p

Saudi Arabia (Dhahran)

Charles M. Thompson
President
American Businessman's Association,
    Eastern Province
P.O. Box 4, Dhahran Airport 31932
Dhahran, Saudi Arabia
Phone:
Telex: 670418 SABSYS SJ

Saudi Arabia (Jeddah)

Bob F. Reece
President
The American Businessmen
    of Jeddah
P.O. Box 5019
Jeddah, Saudi Arabia
Phone: 651-7968
Telex: 401906 UCAJED SJ

Saudi Arabia (Riyadh)

Keith Poulin
Chairman
American Businessmen's Group
  of Riyadh
P.O. Box 8273
Riyadh 11482, Saudi Arabia 07045
Phone: 476-5578
Telex: 204312 DALIL

Singapore

Dorsey Dunn
Chairman
Mobil Oil Singapore
18 Pioneer Road
Jurong Town
Singapore 2262

South Africa

W.J. DeGenring
Managing Director
S.A. Cyanamid (Pty) Ltd.
Elmer Park Center, 1st Floor
Corner 1st Avenue & Adjutant Street
Edenvale, Transvale, South Africa

Spain

Max H. Klein
Max H. Klein y Cia
Pasio de Gracia, 95
Barcelona-8, Spain

Switzerland

J. Quincy Hunsicker
Managing Director
McKinsey & Company
Zollikerstrassa 225
8008 Zurich, Switzerland
Phone: 01/53-44-44
Telex: 55 362

Taiwan

Robert Hoffman
General Manager
General Electric Technical
  Service Company
7F, 201, Tun Hwa North Road
Taipei, Taiwan
Phone: 713-1065/713-6518
Telex: 24529 GEITW

Thailand

Thomas J. White
President
Phelps-Dodge (Thailand) Ltd.
6th Floor, Panunee Building
518/3 Ploenchit Road
Bangkok 10500, Thailand
Phone: 251-2251

United Kingdom

John D. Philipsborn
The Chase Manhattan Bank, NA
Woolgate HSE
Coleman Street
London EC2P 2HD
Phone: (01) 726-5000
Telex: 8954681 CMBG

Uruguay

John Dale
Financial Director
General Motors Uruguay, S.A.
Sayago 1385
Casilla de Correo 234
Montevideo, Uruguay
Phone: 38-16-21/28
Telex: 853

Venezuela

Donald H. Veach
Executive Director and General
Manager
Carton de Venezuela, S.A.
Apartado 609
Caracas 1010, Venezuela
Cable: 25346 CARVEN VC

Regional AMCHAM Organizations
AACCLA

David A. Wicker
President
Association of American Chambers of
  Commerce in Latin America
President
National Distillers do Brasil
Av. Brig. Faria Lima, 4 e 5 andar
01451 Sao Paolo, SP–Brazil
Phone: 813-4133
Telex: 1125635 NOBR BR

APCAC

Warren W. Williams
Chairman
Asia-Pacific Council of American
  Chambers of Commerce
c/o Burston Marsteller
KS Building, 5 Kojimachi, 4-chome
Chiyoda-ku
Tokyo 102, Japan
Phone: (03) 264-6701
Telex: J23242 BMF TYO

European Council

Frederic G. Drake
Chairman
European Council of American
  Chambers of Commerce
President
General Electric–Deutschland
Praunheimer Landstr. 50
6000 Frankfurt 90, West Germany
Phone: 030/34071
Telex: 185820

Appendix D

U.S. EMBASSIES AND EXPORT DEVELOPMENT OFFICES

Regional Export Development Office–Asia/Pacific

7th Floor, World Import Mart
1-3 Higashi Ikebukuro 3-chome
Toshima-ku, Tokyo 170, Japan; of
c/o American Embassy
APO San Francisco 96503
Phone: (03) 987-2441
Telex: 2722446 USTC J
Cable: USTRACEN TOKYO

Export Development Office–Singapore

Unit 1501 Peninsula Plaza
111 N. Bridge Road
Singapore 0617; or
c/o American Embassy
FPO-San Francisco 96699

Export Development Office–Sydney

4 Cliff Street
Milsons Point, Sydney N.S.W. 2061 or
c/o American Embassy
APO San Francisco 96209

Korea Trade Center

U.S. Embassy
82 Sejong-Ro
Chongro-ku
Seoul, Korea or
c/o American Embassy
APO San Francisco 96301
Phone: (822) 722-2601 through 19
Telex: AMEMB 23108

Regional Export Development Office–Europe

U.S. Embassy
Delchmannsaue
5300 Bonn 2
Germany; or
c/o American Embassy
APO New York 0980
Phone: (0228) 339-2081/2
Telex: 08-85-624

Export Development Office–Milan

Via Gattamelata 5
20149 Milan
Italy; or
c/o American Embassy
Box M, APO New York 09794
Phone: 011-392-469-6451

Export Development Office–Vienna

Vienna 1
Schmidgasse 14
A-1080 Vienna, Austria
Phone: 011-43-222-43-21-15
Telex: 116103

International Marketing Center

U.S. Embassy
Grosvenor Square
London W1A 1AE
England or
c/o American Embassy
Box 40, FPO New York 09510

Regional Export Development Office–Middle East/Africa

Room 1510, Code 3340
Office of Event Management and
   Support Services
U.S. Department of Commerce
Washington, D.C. 20230
Phone: 202-377-1209
Telex: 892536 USDOC WSH

Export Development Office–Mexico City

31 Liverpool
Mexico 6, D.F.; or
c/o American Embassy
P.O. Box 3087
Laredo, Texas 78041
Phone: 905/591-0155

Export Development Office–Miami

Suite 100
Springfield Building
8125 N.W. 53rd Street
Miami, Florida 33166 U.S.A.
Phone: 305-350-4913
TWX: 810-848-4187 (ITC DOC MIA)
Cable: RUEVH PG

Export Development Office–Sao Paulo, Brazil

Edificio Eloy Chaves
Avenida Paulista
2439
Sao Paulo, Brazil; or
c/o American Consulate General
APO Miami 34030
Phone: (011) 55-11-853-2011
Telex: (391) 1125274

Appendix E

WORLD BANK OFFICES

Headquarters: 1818 H. Street, N.W. Washington, D.C. 20433, U.S.A.

New York Office: The World Bank Mission to the United Nations/New York Office, 747 Third Avenue (26th Floor), New York, N.Y. 10017, U.S.A.

European Office: The World Bank, 66, avenue d'Iena, 75116 Paris, France

London Office: New Zealand House (15th Floor), London SWI Y4TE, United Kingdom

Geneva Office: The World Bank, ITC Building, 54 Rue de Montbrillant, Geneva, Switzerland (mailing address: P.O. Box 104, 1211 Geneva 20 CIC, Switzerland)

Tokyo Office: The World Bank, Kokusai Building (Room 916), 1-1 Marunouchi 3-chome, Chiyoda-ku, Tokyo 100, Japan

Eastern Africa: The World Bank, Reinsurance Plaza (5th and 6th floors), Taifa Road, Nairobi, Kenya (mailing address: P.O. Box 30577)

Western Africa: The World Bank, Immeuble Shell, 64 Avenue Lamblin, Abidjan 01, Ivory Coast (mailing address: B.P. 1850)

Thailand: The World Bank, Udom Vidhya Building, 956 Rama IV Road, Sala Daeng, Bangkok 5, Thailand

Bangladesh: Resident Mission, The World Bank, 222 New Eskaton Road, Dhaka, Bangladesh (mailing address: G.P.O. Box 97)

Benin: The World Bank, Zone Residentielle de la Radio, Cotonou, Benin (mailing address: B.P. 03-2112)

Bolivia: Banco Mundial, Edificio BISA (4 Piso), 16 de Julio 1628, La Paz, Bolivia (mailing address: Casilla 8692)

Burkina Faso: The World Bank, Immeuble BECEA (3ème étage), Ouagadougou, Upper Volta (mailing address: B.P. 622)

Burundi: The World Bank, 45, Avenue de la Poste, Bujumbura, Burundi (mailing address: B.P. 2637)

Cameroon: The World Bank, Immeuble Kennedy, Avenue Kennedy, Yaounde, Cameroon (mailing address: B.P. 1128)

Colombia: Banco Mundial, Edificio Aseguradora del Valle, Carrera 10, No. 24-55 (Piso 17), Bogota D.C., Colombia (mailing address: Apartado Aereo 10229)

Ethiopia: The World Bank, I.B.T.E. New Telecommunications Building (1st Floor), Churchill Road, Addis Ababa, Ethiopia (mailing address: P.O. Box 5515)

Ghana: The World Bank, 1A Kakramadu Road, East Cantonments, Accra, Ghana (mailing address: P.O. Box M27)

India: Resident Mission, The World Bank, P.O. Box 416, New Delhi, India

Indonesia: Resident Staff in Indonesia, The World Bank, Jalan Rasuna Said, Kav. B-10 (Suite 301), Kuningan, Jakarta 12940, Indonesia (mailing address: P.O. Box 324 JKT)

Madagascar: The World Bank, 1 Rue Patrice Lumumba, Antananarivo 101, Madagascar (mailing address: Banque Mondiale B.P. 4140)

Mali: The World Bank, Immeuble CNAR, rue Square Lumumba, Bamako, Mali (mailing address: B.P. 1864)

Nepal: The World Bank, R.N.A.C. Building (1st Floor), Kathmandu, Nepal (mailing address: P.O. Box 798)

Niger: The World Bank, Immeuble El Nasr (12ème étage–escalier A)Niamey, Niger (mailing address: Banque Mondiale B.P. 12402, c/o Postmaster General)

Nigeria: The World Bank, Plot 1309A, Karim Kotun Street, Victoria Island, Lagos, Nigeria (mailing address: Apartado 4480)

Pakistan: The World Bank, P.O. Box 1025, Islamabad, Pakistan

Peru: Banco Mundial, Avenida Central 643 (1 Piso), Lima, Peru (mailing address: Apartado 4480)

Rwanda: The World Bank, P.O. Box 609, Kigali, Rwanda

Saudi Arabia: Resident Mission, The World Bank, Riyadh, Saudi Arabia (mailing address: P.O. Box 5900)

Senegal: The World Bank, Immeuble S.D.I.H., 3 Place de l'Independence, Dakar, Senegal (mailing address: B.P. 3296)

Somalia: The World Bank, c/o Somali Commercial & Savings Bank Building (4th Floor), Mogadishu, Somalia (mailing address: P.O. Box 1825)

Sri Lanka: The World Bank, People's Bank, Head Office (10th Floor), Sir C.A. Gardiner Mawatha, Colombo 2, Sri Lanka (mailing address: P.O. Box 1761)

Sudan: The World Bank, Sudan Kuwaiti Centre, Tower No. 1 (7th Floor), Nile Avenue, Khartoum, Sudan (mailing address: P.O. Box 2211)

Tanzania: The World Bank, N.I.C. Building (7th Floor, B), Dar es Salaam, Tanzania (mailing address: P.O. Box 2054)

Togo: The World Bank, 169 Boulevard Circulaire, Immeuble BTCI (8eme etage), Lome', Togo (mailing address: B.P. 3915)

Uganda: The World Bank, P.O. Box 4463, Kampala, Uganda

Zaire: The World Bank, Building UZB, Avenue des Aviateurs, Kinshasa 1, Republic of Zaire (mailing address: P.O. Box 14816)

Zambia: The World Bank, CMAZ Building, Ben Bella Road, Lusaka, Zambia (mailing address: P.O. Box 35410)

Zimbabwe: The World Bank, c/o UNDP, UDC Center (3rd floor), 59 Union Avenue-1st Street, Harare, Zimbabwe (mailing address: P.O. Box 4775)

Appendix F

INTER-AMERICAN DEVELOPMENT BANK OFFICES

Argentina

Calle Esmeralda 130, Pisos 19y20
(Casilla de Correo No. 181, Sucursal 1)
Buenos Aires

Bahamas

IBM Building, 4th Floor
(P.O. Box N 3743)
Nassau

Barbados, W.I.

Maple Manor, Hastings
(P.O. Box 402), Christ Church

Bolivia

Edificio "BISA," 5 Piso
Avenida 16 de julio No. 1628
LaPaz

Brazil

Praia do Flamengo N 200, 21 andar
(Caixa Postal 16209, Z0-01)
22210 Rio de Janeiro

Chile

Avenida Pedro de Valdivia 0193,
11 Piso
(Casilla No. 16611,
Correo 9 Providencia)
Santiago

Colombia

Avenida 40 A No. 13-09, 8 Piso
(Apartado Aereo 12037)
Bogotá

Costa Rica

Edificio Centro Colon, Piso 12
Paseo Colon entre Calles 38y40
San Jose

Dominican Republic

Avenida Winston Churchill Esquina
Calle Luis F. Thomen, Torre BHD
(Apartado Postal No. 1386)
Santo Domingo

Ecuador

Avenida Amazonas 477 y Roca
Edificio Banco de los Andes, 9o. Piso
(Apartado Postal 9041-Suc.7)
Quito

El Salvador

Condominio Torres del Bosque
Colonia La Mascota–10 Piso
(Apartado Postal No. (01) 199)
San Salvador

Guatemala

Edificio Geminis 10
12 Calle 1-25, Zona 10, Nivel 19
(Apartado Postal 935), Guatemala

Guyana

47 High Street, Kingston
(P.O. Box 10867), Georgetown

Haiti

Batiment de la banque Nationale de
Paris
Angle de la Rue Lemarre et Calve
(Boite postale 1321), Port-au-Prince

Honduras

Edificio Los Castanos, Pisos 5y6
Colonia Los Castonas
(Apartado Postal No. C-73)
Tegucigalpa

Jamaica

40-46 Knutsford Boulevard, 6th Floor
(P.O. Box 429)
Kingston 10

Mexico

Paseo de la Reforma 379, 7 Piso
Col. Cuauhtemoc
Delegacion Cuauhtemoc
06500 Mexico, D.F.

Nicaragua

Edificio BID
Kilometro 4-1/2 Carretera a Masaya
(Apartado Postal 2512)
Managua

Panama

Avenida Samuel Lewis
Edificio Banco Union, Piso 14
(Apartado Postal 7297)
Panama 5

Paraguay

Edificio Aurora I
Calle Caballero Esquina
Eligio Ayala, Pisos 2 y 3
(Casilla 1209)
Asuncion

Peru

Paseo de la Republica, 3245, 14 Piso
(Apartado Postal No. 3778)
San Isidro, Lima 27

Suriname

Zwartenhoven Brugstraat
32 Boven
Paramaribo

Trinidad and Tobago

Tatil Building, 11 Maraval Road
(P.O. Box 68)
Port of Spain

Uruguay

Andes 1365, 13 Piso
(Casilla de Correo 5029, Sucursal 1)
Montevideo

Venezuela

Nucleo A, Piso 16
Conjunto Miranda
Multicentro Empresarial del Este
Avenida Libertador, Chacao
Caracas 1060

**Institute for Latin American
Integration**

Calle Esmeralda 130–Pisos 16,17,18
(Casilla de Correo No. 39, Sucursal 1)
Buenos Aires

Special Representative in Europe

Reuben Sternfeld
17 Avenue Matignon
75008 Paris, France

Hector E. Luisi
Morgan House
1 Angel Court
London EC2R, 7HJ, United Kingdom

Appendix G

SAMPLE HOUSING AND FURNITURE GUIDELINE

Memo No. 005.374.R2

1. *Scope:* This memorandum states the company policy concerning housing and furniture for members posted overseas.

2. *Purpose:* The purpose of this memo is to standardize and facilitate the provision of housing and furniture for members stationed overseas and to provide a means for normalizing costs of housing and furniture.

3. *Applicability:* This memo applies to overseas members and third national members as defined in Memo No. 005.070. It does not apply to assigned members or local members as defined in Memo No. 005.070.

4. *Basic Policy:* Preferably, members make arrangements for their own housing and furniture, subject to the approval of the Branch, Task Force, or Regional Manager. A *housing allowance*, as outlined below, is established at those posts where this practice is considered practicable by the company. The amount of the allowance is based upon the company's estimate of reasonable cost for housing and furniture, less the cost of similar facilities in Chicago called the "home equivalent." At posts where the use of housing allowance is not practicable in the judgment of the company, housing and furniture is provided in kind by the company, as outlined under *alternate policy.* The member reimburses the company on the basis of reasonable costs of furnishing the facilities in Chicago, designated herein as the "home equivalent."

5. *Housing Allowance:* Housing allowances are established for designated posts by the International Division Head upon recommendation of the Regional Manager in concurrence with Corporate Administration. Allowances are computed on a monthly basis, including:

   a. Approximate rental for a residence of acceptable quality and condition, providing accommodations as set forth below in Paragraph 8.
   b. The approximate purchase cost of "hard" furniture meeting the standards listed in Paragraph 8 amortized over a 60-month period.
   c. 2% of estimated amounts for furniture to cover maintenance and insurance.
   d. Less an amount equal to the "home equivalent" as provided for in Paragraph 7.
   e. Members providing their own housing and furniture are responsible for such lease agreement as may be required and to the lessor for proper utilization and maintenance of the property rented to them.

6. *Alternate Policy:* At posts or on assignments where the use of housing allowance is not practicable in the judgment of the company, housing and furniture is provided in kind by the company and the member pays the company rental on the basis of the "home equivalent" as determined below. When housing and furniture are supplied by the company, the provisions of Paragraphs 8 and 9 apply.

7. *Home Equivalent:* Home equivalent of cost of housing and furniture is computed at 10 percent of base salary. Home equivalent is normally deducted as of the date the member arrives at the assigned post except in cases approved prior to departure, when the member must temporarily maintain two households for family convenience. Home equivalent continues until reassignment to a new post, termination, or such other reason that the member is no longer considered assigned to the post. Home equivalent continues during vacations taken while assigned to the post and during end of tour vacations so long as the member is to return to the post for subsequent assignment.

8. *Facilities Provided:* The company will normally provide housing, furniture, and appliances in accordance with the following:
   a. A member on single status or with wife only: living and dining area, one or two bedrooms, kitchen, and bath. Furniture as listed in Appendix A.
   b. Member with wife and children: living and dining area, kitchen, bath, one master bedroom plus additional bedrooms with the approval of the international division head. Furniture as listed in Appendix A.

9. *Responsibility:* Members are responsible for the safekeeping, maintenance, and proper use of housing, yards, gardens, other related buildings, and furniture and appliances assigned to them. Members meet the cost of all utilities. At the conclusion of occupancy, such facilities are to be returned in the same condition as received, subject only to normal wear and tear. Members are liable for damages to facilities and property caused by negligent or improper use and care.

10. *Effectivity:* This memo is effective as of _____.

11. *Supersedes:* This memo supersedes Memo No. 005.374.R1 dated _____.

Issued by

_____

Date: _____

Attachment to Memo No. 005.374-R2.

Appendix
Company-provided Furniture and Appliances

Kitchen	___ Range, electric, gas, or kerosene
	___ Refrigerator-freezer
	___ Water filter (if required)
	___ Water heater
	___ Work table (if required)
	___ Cupboard (if required)
Laundry	___ Washing machine, clothes dryer
Dining Room	___ Table
	___ Buffet or dish cupboard
	___ Six chairs
Living Room	___ Settee
	___ Two lounge chairs
	___ Coffee table
	___ Two end tables
	___ Two lamps
	___ Table for record player, radio and/or television
	___ Ventilating fan of appropriate size and type
Bedrooms	___ Double or twin beds in master bedroom
	___ One twin bed per child
	___ One chest of drawers per family member
	___ One night table per bed—two per double bed
	___ One lamp per night table
	___ One straight chair per family member
	___ One vanity top and mirror per bedroom
	___ Air conditioner per bedroom if climate dictates (with approval of international division head)
	___ Space heaters, if climate dictates (with approval of international division head)
	___ Provision for hanging clothes, if not built-in closets

Appendix H

Department of State Salary Chart—1987

RATES EFFECTIVE January 4, 1987

Authorized by Executive Order 12578

Executive Schedule/Chief of Mission			Senior Foreign Service/Senior Executive Service		
EX-I: $88,000	EX-IV/COM: $74,500		FE/ES-1: $63,200	FE/ES-4: $70,700	
EX-II: $77,400	EX-V: $70,800		FE/ES-2: $65,700	FE/ES-5: $72,500	
EX-III/COM: $75,800			FE/ES-3: $68,200	FE/ES-6: $74,500	

STEP RATES WITHIN GRADE OR CLASS (DOLLARS)

CATEGORY AND GRADE/CLASS		1	2	3	4	5	6	7	8	9	10	11	12	13	14
GS	FS														
18		86,682*													
17		73,958*	76,423*	78,888*	81,353*	83,818*									
16		63,135	65,240	67,345	69,450	71,555*	73,660*	75,765*	77,870*	79,975*					
15		53,830	55,624	57,418	59,212	61,006	62,800	64,594	66,388	68,182	69,976				
	1	53,830	55,445	57,108	58,821	60,586	62,404	64,276	66,204	68,190	69,976	69,976	69,976	69,976	69,976
14		45,763	47,288	48,813	50,338	51,863	53,388	54,913	56,438	57,963	59,488				
	2	43,619	44,928	46,275	47,664	49,094	50,566	52,083	53,646	55,255	56,913	58,620	60,379	62,190	64,056
13		38,727	40,018	41,309	42,600	43,891	45,182	46,473	47,764	49,055	50,346				
	3	35,344	36,404	37,496	38,621	39,780	40,973	42,203	43,469	44,773	46,116	47,499	48,924	50,392	51,904
12		32,567	33,653	34,739	35,825	36,911	37,997	39,083	40,169	41,255	42,341				
	4	28,640	29,499	30,384	31,296	32,235	33,202	34,198	35,224	36,280	37,369	38,490	39,644	40,834	42,059
11		27,172	28,078	28,984	29,890	30,796	31,702	32,608	33,514	34,420	35,326				
10		24,732	25,556	26,380	27,204	28,028	28,852	29,676	30,500	31,324	32,148				
	5	23,207	23,903	24,620	25,359	26,120	26,903	27,710	28,542	29,398	30,280	31,188	32,124	33,088	34,080
9		22,458	23,207	23,956	24,705	25,454	26,203	26,952	27,701	28,450	29,199				
	6	20,746	21,368	22,009	22,670	23,350	24,050	24,772	25,515	26,280	27,069	27,881	28,717	29,579	30,466
8		20,333	21,011	21,689	22,367	23,045	23,723	24,401	25,079	25,757	26,435				
	7	18,547	19,103	19,677	20,267	20,875	21,501	22,146	22,810	23,495	24,200	24,926	25,673	26,444	27,237
7		18,358	18,970	19,582	20,194	20,806	21,418	22,030	22,642	23,254	23,866				
	8	16,580	17,077	17,590	18,117	18,661	19,221	19,797	20,391	21,003	21,633	22,282	22,951	23,639	24,348
6		16,521	17,072	17,623	18,174	18,725	19,276	19,827	20,378	20,929	21,480				
	9	14,822	15,267	15,725	16,196	16,682	17,183	17,698	18,229	18,776	19,339	19,920	20,517	21,133	21,767
5		14,822	15,316	15,810	16,304	16,798	17,292	17,786	18,280	18,774	19,268				
4		13,248	13,690	14,132	14,574	15,016	15,458	15,900	16,342	16,784	17,226				
3		11,802	12,195	12,588	12,981	13,374	13,767	14,160	14,553	14,946	15,339				
2		10,816	11,073	11,430	11,735	11,866	12,215	12,564	12,913	13,262	13,611				
1		9,619	9,940	10,260	10,579	10,899	11,087	11,403	11,721	11,735	12,036				

*The rate of basic pay payable to employees at these rates is limited to $70,800, the rate payable for Level V of the Executive Schedule.

In his long and distinguished career, H. Peter Guttmann has consulted on development projects throughout the world. A decade ago, he employed his mastery of consulting in the international marketplace to write the first edition of *The International Consultant*. It quickly became *the* leading how-to guide in the field. Now, the author and consultant has updated the book to reflect all the references and statistics in the consulting field that have come into play or that have changed over the past decade.

In this new edition, consultants in engineering, management, architecture, planning, economics, and other related fields will find practical information on expanding their businesses into the world marketplace. *The International Consultant, Revised Edition,* features a region-by-region survey of consulting opportunities around the globe, along with an exploration of the various ways international projects are set up and tested solutions to the problems of staffing, financing, and administration of overseas projects.

Mr. Guttmann offers nuts-and-bolts advice on finding prospects and negotiating contracts abroad, and explains what to expect about contract disputes, arbitration, and termination of contracts. He discusses important issues such as liability, insurance, and bonds and supplies summaries of the policies and practices of 27 international financing agencies—including when and how they hire consultants and how they are most appropriately approached for new business. In the appendix, there is information on the types of agencies in foreign countries with which a consultant is likely to work.